THE MONARCH RETREAT

The Real Life Tales Of Plastic Surgery Clients

By

Sabrina Martin

First published in The United States in 2024 by TEP publishing

12808 West Airport Blvd Suite 270M Sugar Land, TX 77478, Unites States

https://www.theempirepublishers.com/

Our books may be purchased in bulk for promotional, educational, or business use.

Please contact The Empire Publishers at +1 844 636-4579, or by email at support@theempirepublishers.com

First Edition December 2024

This book is dedicated to our amazing staff, many of whom have become lifelong friends, and to our family and friends who helped us get started.

About the Author

Sabrina Martin is a registered nurse and healthcare executive turned entrepreneur and now author.

With a background in business, surgery, and critical care and a love and passion for the beauty industry, Sabrina left corporate America to start a luxury plastic surgery recovery retreat with her husband, encountering unforgettable clients, memories, and unexpected chaos along the way.

Disclaimer

The stories and events presented in this book have been modified to ensure the confidentiality and privacy of our clients.

Table of Contents

Preface

I had just walked out of my corporate office for the last time, adrenaline pulsing through my veins as I stood outside, realizing the magnitude of what I had just done. One moment, I was seated in a boardroom, discussing quarterly earnings with all the enthusiasm of a hamster on a wheel, and the next, I was on the verge of launching the most extravagant plastic surgery recovery retreat Denver had ever seen. The excitement and anxiety were palpable—like stepping onto a high wire without checking the safety net. But what could go wrong, right? The Monarch Retreat was poised to become *the* ultimate sanctuary where post-surgery recovery met five-star luxury, and I was about to lead it all.

But before I get ahead of myself, let me introduce myself properly. I'm Sabrina Martin, your narrator and the mind behind this audacious endeavor. The beauty industry had always been my passion, so when the opportunity to create a retreat for people to recover from their surgeries in sheer style came knocking, I couldn't resist. As a registered nurse working in corporate America, I had always wanted to break away and start something of my own. When I saw the limitless opportunities in the $500 billion beauty industry, I knew I had found my path. I also believe that being a registered nurse would make clients feel safe staying at our retreat. They knew they would be cared for with a level of medical expertise and attention that put their recovery first, all within the lap of luxury. And so, it wasn't just a job for me. It was a chance to build something where passion met purpose [and money, of course].

My husband, Dale, reluctantly joined me on this wild adventure. Funny enough, we didn't meet under glamorous circumstances at all. In fact, our story began in the dull halls of a massive corporate office. After months of awkward workplace banter (the kind HR would raise an eyebrow at), we started dating. Long-distance dating, no less—me in Pennsylvania, him in Colorado. Not exactly the sweeping romance of movies, but it worked.

Eventually, we both made the bold decision to leave our jobs. Dale, ever the cautious one, wasn't fully convinced at first, but I had a grand vision. You see, Colorado is a plastic surgery hotspot, drawing patients from all over the Midwest and Texas to its famed surgeons. And there was a catch. These patients needed somewhere comfortable and discreet to recover. That's where Monarch Retreat came in.

We found the perfect property in what is affectionately known as the "Beverly Hills of Denver." This place was nothing short of opulent—imagine a chef's kitchen, an outdoor kitchen (because why settle for one?), and an elevator to whisk you between floors in the utmost comfort. The upstairs loft? We converted it into a spa, naturally. Post-surgery massages and facials were a must for our clientele, not to mention it added to the indulgence.

Now let's talk about our grand opening. *That* was a spectacle. We invited every plastic surgeon in Denver, and let me tell you, they all showed up. We needed to make a splash, after all. We rolled up in a Jaguar, because subtlety wasn't on the menu that night. And since luxury needs a touch of culture, we partnered with an art studio to fill the walls with pieces worth more than most people's homes. Tens of thousands of dollars in art surrounded recovering clients—it was grand on another level.

But we didn't stop there. A famous Denver chef, who had graced the show *Top Chef,* designed our gourmet recovery menu. Yes, you read that right: *gourmet recovery food.* Our dishes were so indulgent, it almost felt criminal to call it a liquid diet. And, for the record, I still have those recipes tucked away for anyone looking to experience five-star cuisine post-op.

Yet, the crown jewel of Monarch Retreat had to be our medical director. A dear friend of mine, standing at 6'5" with a flamboyant flair for interior design, he brought a unique touch to the place. His impeccable taste elevated the décor to another level, turning the retreat into a dazzling fusion of medical care, luxury spa, and art gallery. We thought we had everything perfectly planned—until the chaos inevitably crept in.

Running a business like this, glamorous as it might sound, was a rollercoaster. There were moments of sheer brilliance and elegance, but also plenty of times when Dale and I exchanged glances, silently asking ourselves, “What have we gotten into?” Between managing high-maintenance clients, keeping an entire staff on track, and navigating Denver’s elite social circles, there was never a dull moment. And don’t even get me started on the delightful marital disagreements that inevitably arose—over everything from gourmet soup recipes to the placement of artwork.

Now, years later, I’m sharing these stories with you—tales of how Monarch Retreat became what it was: a blend of chaos, glamour, and hilarity, with lessons learned along the way. Trust me, you’re in for an unforgettable journey through the world of high-end recovery, where nothing is ever as it seems.

Buckle up, because this book is going to take you on one wild ride.

1

Greek Goddess

When our first client arrived, it was impossible not to notice her. She practically stormed in like a thundercloud, towering over everyone with a presence that commanded attention. She was like something out of a myth—tall, statuesque, with thick black hair that flowed down her back in glossy waves. She looked like a Greek goddess. Not a dainty, delicate figure, but a fierce, sturdy woman who could stand at the helm of a ship in a storm and not blink.

I'd never seen anyone like her, and she was exactly the kind of person you don't forget. When she laughed, which she did often and loudly, her entire body would shake. It wasn't just a laugh, it was an explosion—a deep, bellowing sound that made the walls vibrate and could probably be heard three streets away. Her laughter filled up the room and then some, and when she wasn't laughing, she was giving us what seemed like a never-ending stream of feedback about our business.

She booked two weeks with us, and right away, I wondered if she was planning on staying much longer. Her luggage said she might never leave. There was so much of it! We didn't know what to expect, but we quickly found out that she had opinions on everything, and she was more than happy to share them. It wasn't in a mean or nasty way, but in that blunt, no-nonsense way you'd expect from someone who probably never heard the word "no" in her life. This goddess was a queen of her own world, and she let you know it.

Her reason for staying with us? Recovery. Not just any recovery, though—she had undergone a procedure that, at the time, was brand new and cutting-edge: VASER liposuction. But this wasn't your average fat removal. This procedure was designed to melt away the fat from her abdomen and sculpt it into what looked like a perfect six-pack. Imagine having abs like an Olympic swimmer—rock-hard in appearance but actually soft to the touch. That was the magic of VASER. Her surgeon had done such a good job that we nicknamed him "the waffle iron doc" because her abs had this weird, grid-like look, as if someone had pressed them into a waffle maker and out popped the perfect six-pack.

She was obsessed with her new abs. Every chance she got, she'd lift her shirt, admire herself in the mirror, and strike different poses, tilting her hips like a bodybuilder at a competition. "I look amazing, don't I?" she'd ask, even though she didn't need anyone to answer. She knew she looked fantastic. "I'll have to get my arms and legs done next. I can't have rock-hard abs and flabby arms, can I?" She laughed, but we knew she wasn't kidding. A few months later, she was back for the full-body sculpting.

The recovery, however, was where things got... interesting. The doctor had scheduled her for daily post-op massages, meant to help with swelling and drainage, which seemed routine enough. But her habits outside of the massages were anything but. Dale, my husband, had taken on the role of driver, chef, and sometimes cleaner during this crazy venture of ours. It had started as something he was enjoying, a new kind of adventure, but it quickly became a full-time, exhausting job. Dale would drive her to appointments, make food runs, and, between chauffeuring her to and from her post-op massages, tackle the endless cleaning. We joked that he was like a personal butler, but after a while, the endless cycle of errands started to wear him down.

He knew this was just temporary—until they had enough clients and could hire a full-time staff. Dale, being the business brain of the operation, had already crunched the numbers and pinpointed exactly when that glorious day would come. And let's be honest, it couldn't come soon enough for him! Little did he know, though, that even with a full staff, those extra hats might never fully disappear. Spoiler alert: they tend to linger like that one awkward party guest who never quite gets the hint!

In addition to all of the driving to post op appointments, each day, Dale would be asked to take her to the ATM, where she'd withdraw exactly $500 in cash. Day after day, she'd stuff the money into this huge duffel bag she kept in her room, and it didn't take long before we started to wonder what exactly she was up to. One day, curiosity got the better of me, and I asked why she needed to withdraw such specific amounts of cash every day.

"I run my own business," she said with a nonchalant wave. "There's a certain amount of money I need to take out each day." She said it as if it were the most normal thing in the world, like brushing your teeth or walking the dog. I didn't press further, but her answer definitely didn't satisfy my curiosity. If anything, it only made me more curious. And then, things got even stranger.

One afternoon, I went to check on her post-op progress, as part of our routine. I knocked, stepped inside, and there she was—lounging on the bed with her laptop open in front of her. But it wasn't the lounging that caught my attention. She was mid-process, creating what looked like a passport on the screen. I blinked, not quite sure if I was seeing things correctly. She didn't seem fazed by my entrance at all. In fact, she looked up and smiled as if we were having a casual conversation over coffee.

"Oh, don't worry," she said, clearly noticing the shock on my face. "I make fake IDs for people. It's no big deal."

No big deal? I had just walked in on her casually crafting an illegal document, and she was acting like it was nothing! She went on to explain that she'd been living under a fake name for years, often in all different parts of the world. I couldn't help but wonder why she was telling me all of this, but then it dawned on me—it must've been the pain meds. She was completely loose-lipped, revealing secrets she'd probably never admit otherwise. After the initial shock wore off, I had to laugh. Here we were, running a nice little recovery business, and our first client was living under an alias, making fake passports, and stashing cash.

We joked amongst ourselves that we had a real-life 007 staying with us. And in some ways, she was. Everything about her screamed wealth and mystery. The diamond rings on her fingers, the designer clothes she wore, and of course, the fact that she'd spent a whopping $50,000 on surgery to carve out abs that most people would only dream of.

Then there was the issue of post-op "leakage." No one had warned us about how much someone would ooze after surgery like hers, and we learned this lesson the hard way. We had been transporting her around in our immaculate white Jaguar with light gray leather seats. What a mistake. Every time she got out of the car, it looked like a crime scene. We were sure the car wash attendants thought we were involved in something dark and illegal. Our Jaguar practically lived at the car wash, going in for a deep clean so often I started to wonder if they had a special "blood and fluids" loyalty program—Dale certainly seemed like their VIP member. Every time he pulled up to the car wash, you could see the exhaustion creeping in. Between the endless chauffeuring and scrubbing mystery stains out of the leather seats, the poor guy was starting to look like the human version of a dried-out sponge.

If that wasn't enough, she also had an appetite that rivaled her grand personality. On her first day post-op, she requested a cheeseburger. Now, I knew that greasy, high-fat, high-salt food was definitely not recommended after surgery, so I hesitated. But she was insistent. Still, I called her doctor for clearance, expecting him to shut the idea down. Instead, his response floored me.

"Sure," he said, "feed her burgers. It's good for business—she'll be back sooner for more surgery."

I was speechless. But sure enough, we got her the burger and fries, and she devoured it with gusto. No regrets, no second thoughts. The more I got to know her, the less I was surprised by anything she did.

And then, there was the spandex suit. After her surgery, she had to wear a tight compression garment to hold everything in place while her body healed. This wasn't just any spandex—it was like a full-body corset, with what felt like a thousand tiny hooks that had to be meticulously clasped shut.

It was a picture to behold. Me, just over five feet tall and a hundred twenty pounds, trying to wrangle this six-foot-two Greek goddess into a suit that looked like it belonged to a child. It was a sight. The first time I had to help her into it, I nearly broke a sweat. I could feel my arms shaking as I fastened each hook, one by one, trying not to laugh at the absurdity of the situation. She, of course, found it hilarious, throwing her head back and laughing so hard she almost tipped over.

"You're stronger than you look!" she'd bellow as I fumbled with the last few hooks. By the time I finished, I felt like I'd run a marathon. But it didn't stop there. Every day, I had to help her back into that suit, and every day, I braced myself for the workout. My arms ached, my back was sore, but it was all part of the job. After a while, it became a kind of routine. We'd laugh together as I struggled with the spandex, and I'd check her surgical areas to make sure everything was healing properly.

We knew running a surgical recovery retreat would be hard work, but we were blindsided by all the *extra* duties beyond the normal post-op care. Turns out, we weren't just caregivers—we were also therapists, friends, and your personal "whatever you need, whenever you need it" service, all wrapped up in one. Not exactly what we thought we signed up for! But hey, for now, we had to keep our eyes on the prize: more clients, a full retreat, and the glorious path to financial freedom... and maybe, just maybe, less impromptu therapy sessions!

But despite the oddities and challenges, she was **unforgettable.** She gave us more than just her business; she gave us stories we'd be telling for years. By the time she left, cash-stuffed duffel bag in tow, we felt like we'd survived a wild initiation into the world of post-op recovery. She eventually returned for more sculpting, more cheeseburgers, and more adventures, and each time she walked through our doors, we knew one thing for sure: life with the Greek Goddess was never, ever boring.

2

Cherry Creek Aristocrat

We didn't exactly expect this client to need much attention. After all, she was coming in for an elective surgery—a tummy tuck, nothing life-threatening. We assumed she'd be in, get pampered a little, and be back out in no time. Little did we know that this glamorous woman, with her carefully constructed appearance and seemingly endless resources, would have us scrambling between gourmet meals, post-surgery cleanup, and emotionally charged moments that made us rethink our entire business model.

Our day began like any other, except this time, we hadn't had the pleasure of meeting our new guest beforehand. When we arrived to pick her up after her surgery, we were introduced to her surgeon—a guy who split his time between Beverly Hills and Denver, kind of like a plastic surgery ninja, appearing wherever the rich and fabulous needed a tuck or lift. This guy was practically the Don King of the plastic surgery world. And our guest was a striking woman in her 60s, whose face was tight—*too* tight for her age, like a perfect canvas that hadn't caught up with the rest of her body.

When she climbed into the car, there was no small talk, no post-surgery giggles. She was quiet, reserved, and a bit out of it, which was understandable given she had just undergone a major surgery under anesthesia. We brought her back to our recovery sanctuary and checked her into our finest room, the Lavender and Lily room. All our rooms had names, but this one was special. It boasted a giant portrait of a lily, something borrowed from a local art gallery, with a $40K price tag. It was a massive canvas that took up the entire wall—so big, we were practically praying no one in a spandex suit full of drainage would accidentally back into it! Honestly, every time one of our post-op guests wandered near it, we found ourselves holding our breath, just hoping the artwork would survive the recovery process without becoming an unfortunate casualty!

I tucked her into bed, making sure she was comfortable and in the proper post-op position. We had splurged on adjustable luxury mattresses, thinking this would be the height of pampering, but she wasn't exactly feeling like a queen. She asked me, in a soft voice that felt a little too fragile for someone who just underwent surgery, not to leave. She didn't want to be alone. That's when it hit me—the loneliness. There was something in her tone that wasn't just groggy from anesthesia; it was almost fearful. I sat with her for a while, holding her hand until she drifted off to sleep. This was the moment I realized we weren't just offering a place for physical recovery, but something more—something like emotional therapy with a side of fresh linens.

* * *

I was under this wild assumption that people coming in for elective surgeries would be low-maintenance. How naïve I was. You'd think that someone choosing to go under the knife would be chill, right? You know, they'd sleep through the night, wake up refreshed, and only need the occasional refill of ice water. Oh no, my friend. This woman taught me that elective surgery clients are *high-maintenance*. I'm talking 'ring the bell every hour' kind of high-maintenance.

Our bell system was cute in theory—just a little ring to summon us when needed. But since our staff consisted of... well, Dale and me, it became the world's worst relay race. It felt like every time we sat down for a breather, we heard the familiar *ding*, and we'd have to spring back into action.

Whether it was a pillow adjustment, a drink of water, or—my personal favorite—ice cubes, she kept us on our toes.

It became clear that Dale was starting to crack. He'd been the chauffeur, chef, and now part-time butler. And you know what? He never signed up for any of this. The man just wanted to make filet mignon and pretend he was on "Top Chef." Even though we hired one of Denver's top chefs to create the menu, we definitely couldn't afford him whipping up every meal. So, Dale had to become his apprentice, which basically meant learning to play 'MasterChef' in real time. Suddenly, Dale's in the kitchen, turning out brioche French toast with warm strawberry compote, house-made whipped cream, and a cappuccino... for breakfast. Really? We were just hoping he wouldn't burn toast, and here we are, running a five-star brunch spot! He was practically living out the worst episode of "Downton Abbey" where the butler also doubles as the cook and the maid.

Speaking of filet mignon, let's talk about her post-surgery dinner. Now, we didn't have a full-time chef—couldn't afford one. But we *did* have a menu designed by a famous chef, and Dale, followed the recipes like his life depended on it. Our guest was thrilled at the idea of having a chef-prepared meal. She practically lit up when we served her steak, mashed potatoes, and some fancy greens on the side. You would've thought she was dining at a Michelin-starred restaurant with the way she raved about it. And, well, this time she kinda was! We actually had this high-priced celebrity chef whip up dinner, not just to impress her (she rolled in some pretty influential social circles) but also the doc who moonlighted in Beverly Hills. These were exactly the kind of clients we thought we wanted to impress—and hopefully capitalize on!

Now, what they don't tell you when you're learning the ropes of post-op care is how dangerous filet mignon can be. About an hour after dinner, our guest started to look a little green. Then it happened—the filet made its grand reappearance, only this time all over our precious Lily painting. I'll never forget Dale's face when he walked into the room and saw the aftermath. His jaw dropped and he became an even more horrific shade of green than mine.

"Is this... is this *on* the painting?" he stammered.

"Yep. All over it," I replied, trying to remain calm but feeling the panic rise.

The $40K lily now had an unfortunate garnish, and we had no idea how to clean a work of art without ruining it. There's no chapter in the post-op care manual titled *How to Scrub Expensive Paintings Without Destroying Them.* Dale and I spent a good hour meticulously cleaning the painting, and by some miracle, we managed to save it. Though, I'm pretty sure we aged 10 years in the process.

That night, it wasn't just the painting that had me on edge—it was everything. If you've ever thrown up after a tummy tuck (or C-section), you know it's like being in a horror movie you can't escape from. So there I was, not only cleaning her up and rubbing her back, telling her everything was going to be fine, but also frantically hunting down her anti-nausea meds like my life depended on it. Her fancy 5-course meal? Reduced to saltine crackers and ginger ale in a matter of minutes. The rest of the night was spent checking on her every hour, and I felt so guilty, like it was my terrible judgment that had caused it all.

The next day, she seemed much more stable, but her emotional needs didn't wane. In fact, they deepened. On one particularly quiet afternoon, she asked me to accompany her back to her house to pick up a few personal items. Of course, I agreed, and we made the trip to her estate.

Now, when I say estate, I mean this place looked like a governor's mansion. It had these towering white pillars, lush grounds, and an air of grandeur that screamed "old money." As she led me through the house, showing me priceless paintings, sculptures, and antique furniture, I couldn't help but be in awe. It was like stepping into a royal palace, minus the army of butlers and maids quietly handling everything in the background.

But the house was cold. Not just physically, but emotionally. There was a stillness, a kind of emptiness that made me realize why she had clung to us so much during her recovery. The place was stunning, sure, but it was also eerily quiet. She had no children, and her husband was apparently always away on business. It was like being in a beautiful museum with no one to share it with. The loneliness she had shown me in the Lavender and Lily room wasn't just post-surgery vulnerability—it was the kind of loneliness that had been her companion for years.

* * *

What was supposed to be a one-night stay turned into a week-long retreat. She kept ringing the bell, and we kept showing up. There were moments when Dale and I would exchange exhausted glances, wondering how much more we could take. But then, in quieter moments, when I sat with her in the Lavender and Lily room, I could see the gratitude in her eyes. She needed this time—needed us, even if we were just two slightly overwhelmed caretakers playing multiple roles. It wasn't just the surgery recovery; it was the emotional recovery too.

Over time, I started to feel for her in ways I hadn't expected. Sure, she was high-maintenance and had the occasional filet-related catastrophe, but she was also just... lonely. And in the weirdest way, that loneliness bound us together during her stay. Dale still grumbled about the endless bell ringing, but I think even he realized that for her, it wasn't about needing fresh ice cubes—it was about knowing someone was there.

By the time she left, we were both exhausted, but there was a weird sense of accomplishment too. We had survived a week of bell-ringing, steak mishaps, and expensive painting rescues, but more importantly, we had made a difference. She had walked into our lives as a tightly pulled woman who seemed to have it all, and left with a little more light in her eyes—less because of the tummy tuck and more because she knew someone had cared enough to sit with her.

As for Dale? Well, let's just say he's still a little traumatized by the painting incident, and he hasn't cooked filet mignon since. But we learned that this whole business wasn't just about physical recovery—it was about healing in all forms, even if that meant bringing a little warmth to someone who had more money than companionship.

3

Benjamin Button

By the time *he* rolled into our retreat, we had already been open for several months, and things were starting to hum along. We had clients pouring in, hired a few staff, and even had contracts with some of the top plastic surgeons in town. They were including our retreat as the *go-to* place for post-op recovery. Business was booming, the rooms were filling up, and we were finally seeing some profit. We were flying high.

Then along came our Wyoming cattle rancher—midlife crisis in full swing.

***

I'll never forget the day he arrived. There I was, checking the retreat schedule and seeing "Wyoming Cattle Rancher" listed as our next client. It seemed like an odd detail to include, but I soon understood why. The man—let's call him John —drove up in a huge monster pickup truck- the kind of truck that costs well over 6 figures, Wyoming plates proudly clinging to the bumper. When he stepped out, he looked like something straight out of *Yellowstone*. Tall, rugged, handsome, in a way that made you think he'd spent his whole life wrangling cattle and fighting off grizzlies. He wore faded Wrangler jeans, boasted a huge belt buckle, and a plain white tee, this man knew how to rock the ranch look.

The kicker? He reached into the back of his truck and pulled out a *giant* cooler of grass-fed beef filets and burgers on ice—like the largest amount of beef I've ever seen in my life. Was he bringing this as a gift? His meals? I immediately began having flashbacks to the filet mignon evening. All of a sudden, I found myself wondering: *Why is this guy even here?* I mean, he looked pretty fit—flat abs, strong arms—so what exactly did he want to change?

***

Little did we know, John had already been in town making all sorts of *cosmetic* plans. Apparently, the guy had gone on a consultation spree and lined up *multiple* procedures for one epic day. We're talking a marathon of vanity surgeries, all spearheaded by the same surgeon—whom we affectionately referred to as Dr. Waffle Iron. (The same doctor who worked on our Greek Goddess.)

John's grand transformation started with VASER liposuction to give him those coveted six-pack abs. The guy already had a pretty flat stomach, but hey, why not aim for Greek god status? Next up was a fat transfer to his face (and yes, that meant taking fat from his butt and injecting it into his face—gives new meaning to the term "buttface," doesn't it?). As if that wasn't enough, he also had an upper blepharoplasty—basically getting rid of his sagging eyelids, so he wouldn't look so "tired." All by our good friend Dr. Waffle Iron and a couple of his close associates.

But the day wasn't over. After hours of surgery, when we picked him up—groggy, barely coherent, looking like he'd been hit by a truck—we were informed that he had one more stop to make. Another clinic specialized in hair plugs, and John wasn't about to miss that appointment. He had a full head of hair, but apparently, that *slight* receding hairline in the front was just too much to handle. So, back under sedation he went, for another two hours.

By the time we picked him up again, he looked... well, he looked like an entirely different person. Or rather, like a swollen, stitched-up version of his former self. With his hair freshly plugged, his face puffed up from the fat injections, and his abs wrapped in a skin-tight compression suit, he resembled a strange combination of a baby and a superhero whose powers had gone terribly wrong.

* * *

When we got him back to the retreat and settled him into his room, all we could do was stare at him in disbelief. Here was a guy who had walked in looking like a rugged, handsome 50-something, and now he looked like an inflated balloon version of himself. His face was so swollen, he barely had any expression, and the compression suit was practically suctioned to his torso like a second skin.

I kept wondering, *What was the end result going to look like?* Because at that moment, it sure looked like he'd made a huge mistake. He went from a handsome, rugged cowboy to a swollen, bewildered baby-man in less than 24 hours.

***

As John slowly recovered over the next few days, he started panicking. And I mean *full-on* panic. Not because of the pain or the swelling—no, John had bigger worries. Like, *how was he going to explain this to the boys back home in Wyoming*?

Turns out, John wasn't just here for a glow-up—he was trying to win back his soon-to-be ex-wife, who had been having an affair. His plan was to transform himself into the man of her dreams, but now that he looked 20 years younger (or at least would eventually), he realized that the folks back in Wyoming were never going to let him live it down. A cattle rancher getting plastic surgery? He'd never hear the end of it.

That's when John, in his post-op haze, came up with the most elaborate cover story I've ever heard. One day, while I was checking his vitals and changing his dressings, he proudly announced, "I've got it! I know what I'm gonna tell everyone!"

His grand idea? Oh, it was a masterpiece. He'd tell people he was out horseback riding in the Colorado Rockies, living his best rugged, outdoorsy life, when disaster struck. Apparently, he stumbled upon a hiker and their dog, and the horse, in true dramatic fashion, freaked out like it had seen a ghost. Next thing you know, John is being bucked off like a cowboy in a rodeo and flying 20 feet down the side of a cliff, all *grace* and *dignity*, of course. His face? Well, it got a little...rearranged. But by pure luck, the hiker just happened to be your average, everyday plastic surgeon who, consumed with guilt over the whole thing, decided to fix John's face *for free.* A total Hallmark moment.

I had to bite my lip to keep from laughing. The story was so far-fetched, it bordered on ridiculous, but hey, what did I know about Wyoming ranch boys and their level of gullibility? He even asked me to pose for a picture with him in my scrubs, so he could prove to his friends and family that he had a nurse taking care of him during his *recovery from the accident.* At that point, I figured, why not? It wasn't the strangest thing I'd done that week.

***

During his two-week stay, John became somewhat of a fixture at the retreat. It was still just me, my friend Courtney (our first employee and a certified nursing assistant), and my husband Dale. We got used to his quirky demeanor, and soon enough, we developed a bit of a friendship.

Courtney and I would chat with him during his check-ups, and despite the fact that he looked like a confused, swollen version of his former self, he had a good sense of humor about it all. John even invited us to come visit Wyoming when we got the chance, assuring us that there was plenty of room at the ranch, where we could ride horses into the sunset without any horrible accidents.

We watched as the swelling in his face slowly subsided, his abs started taking shape, and the new hairline finally settled in. By the end of his stay, John was starting to resemble his original self—albeit with a few upgrades. He left the retreat looking like a much younger, smoother version of the man who had first walked in, and while we were happy to see him go, we were a little sad too. He had become a part of our little retreat family.

***

A few months later, we got a letter from John. He was back in Wyoming, his horseriding story had worked like a charm (to our surprise), and he was doing just fine. He had gotten divorced, but somehow, he hadn't lost any friends. Oh, and he had a new girlfriend. I couldn't help but wonder just how much younger she was, but that's none of my business, right?

So there you have it. The Wyoming cattle rancher's midlife crisis makeover, complete with a crash course in plastic surgery, a ridiculous cover story, and a freezer full of beef that lasted us for months on end.

4

Dark and Stormy

It was a night to remember—a night when the universe conspired against us in ways we could never have anticipated. The retreat had been open for over a year by this point, but we were far from cruising along. Despite our grand plans of running this multi-million-dollar estate like a chic, glamorous bed and breakfast, it was slowly dawning on us that we weren't living in luxury. No, this was more like living in a 24/7 psych ward disguised as a medical spa. And on this particular stormy night, it felt like the place had turned into the set of a horror movie—complete with a haunted house, chaotic screaming, and mysterious arrivals. But I digress; let me take you back to the beginning of that unforgettable evening.

The sky had been threatening all day, but we had foolishly hoped the weather would cooperate. Silly us. By dusk, the wind was howling like it was auditioning for a remake of *Twister*, and rain poured down in torrents. It was the kind of night where you just knew something bizarre was about to happen, and sure enough, it did.

We were over capacity. Again. Despite having both a day crew and a night crew on staff, we were still running around like headless chickens, trying to keep the place from descending into complete madness. We had even converted our own sleeping quarters into makeshift client rooms. Yes, you heard that right. What we had originally envisioned as a charming setup, where we would one day own and live in this fabulous estate, had become a complete nightmare. We were basically living at work, and on nights like these, it felt like the work was trying to eat us alive.

Our last resort was to sleep in the loft spa, which sounds fancy in theory. But let me tell you, when you've got a cacophony of clients buzzing their emergency call buttons every 15 minutes, it's anything but relaxing. So, in a last-ditch attempt to preserve our sanity, we grabbed our pillows and blankets and camped outside on the deck by the fire. Yes, you read that right: *camping*. In the rain. By the fire. While our staff inside tried to manage the chaos. It was like a scene out of some twisted survival reality show—*The Great Clinic Escape*, or *When Surgeons Attack*.

And then came the call.

Courtney, my brave and perpetually overworked right hand, was the one to answer it. I watched her face go pale as she listened to whoever was on the other end of the line. This was never a good sign.

"We're full," she said, trying to hold her ground. "I'm sorry, but we don't have any rooms left."

Pause.

Then she looked at me, eyes wide with alarm. "They want to talk to you," she whispered, handing me the phone like it was a live grenade.

I should have known right then that nothing good was about to happen, but I picked up the phone, hoping for a miracle. Instead, I got a frantic voice explaining that their patient's surgery had gone way longer than expected, and he was bleeding a lot. He needed to be monitored overnight, and there was *literally* nowhere else for him to go.

"We have no rooms," I reiterated, trying to make it clear that we were not, in fact, running the Four Seasons.

“We’ll take the living room,” the voice replied, as if this were a perfectly reasonable solution to the problem of zero available beds.

I blinked, momentarily stunned. The *living room*? You want to rest this poor man in the *living room*? We had some spare zero-gravity chairs that our tummy-tuck clients occasionally used to lounge on the deck, but that’s not exactly high-end post-op care.

“Fine,” I said finally. “But you have to pick him up in the pouring rain.”

Of course, poor Courtney, who had been hoping to go home to her kids, ended up being the one to brave the storm and retrieve this catastrophe of a patient.

* * *

I was sitting by the fire when the front door of the retreat swung open, and in walked what can only be described as a scene straight out of a horror movie. A man, drenched from head to toe, shuffled in wearing a black hoodie that might as well have come straight from the wardrobe department of *Psycho*. His face—well, what we could see of it—was swollen beyond recognition, with bandages crisscrossing over his cheeks, and two drains hanging from either side, each one filled with more blood than I was emotionally prepared to handle at that moment.

I stood there, half expecting him to moan "It's alive!" as thunder cracked in the background. Courtney, bless her heart, was already regretting her life choices as she helped him shuffle into the living room, where the zero-gravity chair awaited his impending collapse.

And collapse he did.

What followed was one of the longest nights of my life. The poor man was completely disoriented, not having the faintest idea where he was or why he was there. Every time I left his side for even a minute, he'd start screaming like a banshee. At one point, he threw a water bottle across the room, narrowly missing a vase we'd recently bought to make the retreat feel more "homey."

"Take your Ativan," I kept whispering like some sort of exhausted drug pusher. "It'll help you relax."

But this guy was a real piece of work. He wasn't just swollen; he was practically bursting at the seams. His face looked like someone had tried to stuff a turkey and then abandoned the process halfway through. According to his records, he'd undergone what was supposed to be a "mini" facelift—a quick, in-and-out procedure. No anesthesia required, they said! What they didn't say was that the doctors at the clinic had learned their technique on oranges (yes, actual oranges) during their certification. You see, it is legal to perform a face lift on someone and NOT be a board-certified plastic surgeon- just simply trained and signed off as a certification. So moral of the story here- always do your research- extensive research- before going under the knife!

And let me tell you, there's nothing "mini" about five hours of hacking away at someone's face with no anesthesia. He was a swollen, confused, and very, very unhappy camper.

***

As the night dragged on, I began to lose track of time. The rain outside continued to lash against the windows, the storm seemingly never-ending. Inside, our retreat had turned into a house of horrors. The other clients—who, I might add, had paid a small fortune for their facelifts—were peering out of their rooms, probably wondering if we had decided to start a side business as a haunted attraction.

Meanwhile, our latest arrival was still trying to make sense of his situation. "Why am I in the living room?" he asked at one point, as if he hadn't noticed the zero-gravity chair he was perched on. "Is this where I'm supposed to be?"

"Yes," I said, deadpan. "Doctors' orders."

He looked at me, bewildered, but accepted it without question. He was too swollen and too sedated to argue.

Around 3 a.m., things finally started to calm down. He had stopped screaming long enough to realize that he was safe (relatively speaking), and I had iced his face so many times that I was beginning to wonder if I should just tape an ice pack directly to his head.

***

By morning, the storm had passed, and with it, some of the chaos. Our patient—let's call him Frank as in short for Frankenstein (poor thing) —had finally stopped bleeding and was no longer screaming like a lost soul. He even thanked us, though his gratitude was marred slightly by a comment that I'm sure was intended as a joke but hit a little too close to home.

"So, I paid $600 to sleep in your living room all night?" he asked, a bemused expression crossing his swollen face.

"Yes," I said flatly. "Doctors' orders."

We all laughed, but deep down, I was thinking: *I didn't sign up for this.* This was supposed to be a luxurious, upscale recovery retreat. Not a place where we end up sleeping on the deck and offering post-op care in the living room because we're overbooked.

Looking back, it's hard not to laugh at the absurdity of it all. We had grand dreams of running this recovery retreat like a glamorous bed and breakfast, but the reality was far from that. We were living in a constant state of chaos, trying to manage the unpredictable nature of these various surgeries and their even more unpredictable aftermath.

That night was a turning point—one that made us realize we had bitten off more than we could chew. But like any good horror movie, we survived. And in the light of day, it's all just part of the legend of one man surviving the 'Fast Food of Facelifts'.

If nothing else, we now know: never trust a surgeon who's learned facelifts on an orange. And always, always have extra zero-gravity chairs on hand—you never know when you'll need them.

5

The Lunch Party

It was a calm Wednesday morning when the call came in. Another one of Dr. Beverly Hills' specials—a client from the Cherry Creek elite—was en route to our retreat for post-op recovery. Now, if you've never met a Cherry Creek socialite, let me paint you a picture: they're the sort who treat a surgical procedure like a spa day and expect to leave looking like they've spent the week at the Ritz. And our latest client was no different. Her name? Let's call her *Clarissa VanDuchess*—because honestly, the real name might have been just as ridiculous.

Clarissa was one of those women whose presence announced itself long before she ever opened her mouth. We hadn't had the pleasure of meeting her prior to her surgery, but we'd heard plenty. She lived in the wealthiest pocket of town, rolled with the highest of society, and threw dinner parties so lavish they made Gatsby look like an amateur.

From the moment we picked her up at the Beverly Hills clinic, I knew we were in for a ride. She was tall—statuesque, really—at least six feet in heels, and with a body that seemed sculpted by a team of artisans, rather than a surgeon. She floated into the retreat, her flawless porcelain skin practically glowing under the soft lighting. Not an ounce of fat on her, and yet here she was, fresh off a tummy tuck and breast lift. I couldn't help but wonder what exactly the doctor had "tucked." She was the kind of person who could make you feel like an overstuffed pillow just standing next to her.

We escorted her to the Blue Lagoon suite, our prized room reserved for the VIPs—quiet, isolated, and on the lowest level of the retreat. It was perfect for someone who needed privacy and rest. Of course, I thought she would spend her first day sleeping off the anesthesia and pain meds, but I underestimated Clarissa. After getting her settled with ice water, a fluffy pillow, and a generous helping of post-op painkillers, I figured she was set for the night. That's when I made the rookie mistake of thinking this was going to be an easy one.

When I went back to check on her later, I found her standing in front of the full-length mirror in nothing but her underwear and surgical bra, admiring herself like she was about to step out onto a runway. Her eyes were a little glassy, and she was swaying ever so slightly, slurring her words as she gazed at her own reflection.

"Don’t I look fabulous?" she asked, her voice dripping with satisfaction. "I think I’m already thinner."

I blinked. She’d had the surgery *yesterday*. Her body hadn’t even started healing, let alone showing results, but here she was, convinced she was ready for her close-up.

***

The next morning, things took a turn. I had barely finished my first coffee when Clarissa strolled into the kitchen, looking as radiant as ever—minus the bandages—and dropped the bombshell.

“I’m hosting a lunch today,” she said, with all the nonchalance of someone ordering a latte.

"Excuse me?" I choked out, half-laughing because surely she was joking.

"Oh, just a little lunch. Six people, nothing big. I've invited some friends." She waved her hand as if summoning six people to a medical recovery retreat for an impromptu luncheon was something we dealt with on a daily basis.

Now, our retreat did offer a clause that allowed clients to have visitors, but we'd never had someone actually take us up on it—let alone to the extent of throwing a full-blown lunch party. Most of the time, we'd get a visitor or two who would stop by with a few well-wishes, have a cup of tea, and be on their way. But Clarissa wasn't one to do things by halves. No, she was the kind of woman who would turn even a hangnail into a red-carpet affair.

Dale, my husband and our retreat's reluctant top chef, nearly fainted when I told him about the luncheon. He had already been running on fumes, cooking gourmet meals for our recovering clientele—who still expected filet mignon even with their faces bandaged and jaws wired shut. Dale took pride in his work, but this was a bit much, even for him.

"What do you mean six people?!" he gasped, his face turning a lovely shade of panic.

"Six, Dale. Six Cherry Creek elites. It's basically a review board for us," I replied, grimacing. "We can't afford a bad review, especially now that the retreat's finally filling up."

Poor Dale. While I sent our staff out on a grocery run, he began furiously prepping, sweating over every detail like a Michelin-star chef on his worst day. The Royal Eggplant–the name we had given our common dining area–had never seen such an occasion. If there was any place destined to be reviewed by Denver's crème de la crème, this was it. And Clarissa's crowd wasn't exactly known for leniency when it came to service.

***

By 1 p.m., the royal luncheon was in full swing. Clarissa had insisted on greeting her guests like a seasoned hostess–despite the fact she had just undergone surgery and was already two mimosas deep by the time they arrived. It didn't help that she was sneaking mini-bottles of something much stronger into her juice when she thought no one was looking.

I'd caught her once, trying to subtly pour a mini-bottle of vodka into her orange juice behind a potted plant. I informed her, of course, that alcohol wasn't recommended after surgery and especially not with pain meds. She gave me a half-lidded look and said, "Dr. Beverly Hills said it was fine. Just a couple drinks, darling."

Something told me Dr. Beverly Hills had said no such thing, but after calling his office, to my shock, his assistant confirmed, "As long as she's limiting it to a couple drinks, it should be fine." My hands were tied at this point. So, I just hoped for the best and braced myself for whatever chaos would follow.

Clarissa's guests were everything you'd expect—dressed in designer labels, gliding into the retreat as if they'd just walked off the set of *Real Housewives.* The men were impeccably dressed in tailored suits, and the women? Not a hair out of place, not a wrinkle in sight. They even brought a bottle of Bordeaux so expensive I felt like I needed insurance just to hold it. I hesitated before decanting it, but Clarissa's permission had opened Pandora's wine bottle.

I couldn't help but marvel at the sheer absurdity of it all. These people were here to visit their friend who had just been stitched up like a human doll, and yet, they were treating it like a luncheon at the country club. There was no concern for her well-being, no "How are you feeling?" Instead, they launched straight into discussions of their latest investments, vacation homes in Tuscany, and the woes of hiring "decent" household staff. It was a veritable contest of who could sound more disgustingly rich.

Dale, meanwhile, was a one-man orchestra in the kitchen. He whipped up appetizers, lunch entrees, and desserts like a man possessed. If there was a stove Olympics, Dale would have taken gold, despite the fact that his back had already started giving out. As the conversation in the dining area grew more artificial and self-indulgent, Dale was battling his own personal war in the kitchen, muttering curses under his breath as he plated seared salmon and truffled risotto.

***

By the time dessert was served, Dale was practically hunched over in agony, and Clarissa's friends were well into their third bottle of wine. The conversation had turned to politics—a surefire way to ruin any meal—but they carried on with the air of people who believed their opinions were not only correct, but should be enshrined in law. Not once did they ask Clarissa how she was doing or whether she was in pain. They didn't even offer a thank you as Dale and I served them dish after dish.

Three hours passed, and finally—mercifully—the luncheon drew to a close. Clarissa's guests made their grand exit, leaving behind a trail of empty wine glasses and half-hearted compliments about how "quaint" the retreat was. Dale, barely able to stand, collapsed into a chair as soon as they left. He'd put his back out for real this time, and it would take a week of muscle relaxers and bed rest for him to recover.

But as much as we wanted to forget the whole ordeal, Clarissa wouldn't let us. Later that night, I found her once again in front of the mirror, wearing only her underwear and bra, surrounded by a sea of empty mini-bottles. She swayed slightly as she turned this way and that, admiring her still-swollen figure.

"Look at me," she said, her voice thick with a blend of alcohol and satisfaction. "Don't I look incredible?"

I stared at her for a moment, speechless. Here was this woman—an aristocrat by all measures—standing in front of her reflection, marveling at a body that was barely holding itself together. She didn't seem to notice the bandages, the swelling, or the fact that her insides had been rearranged like furniture in a showroom. She was utterly and completely in love with her own image, mini-bottles be damned.

The next morning, she left us a glowing review. "Exquisite service, five-star meals, and the best recovery experience ever," she wrote. "I felt like royalty."

And honestly, that's all that mattered.

6

The Double Ds

Our retreat has welcomed an array of clients, each bringing a unique blend of quirks, preferences, and often, peculiar post-surgical needs. Over the years, we'd grown used to handling everything from soothing frazzled nerves to managing surprise side effects. But nothing, absolutely nothing, prepared us for the whirlwind that was Ms. Double Ds.

Ms. Double Ds was the kind of client who strutted through the door with the air of someone carrying the world's best-kept secret. Her newfound enthusiasm practically radiated off her, beaming brighter than our lobby's accent lighting. With every enthusiastic sway, she reminded us that her 400cc implants were not merely cosmetic enhancements; they were her newest life upgrades. Her entry was like the start of a new reality show episode, and little did we know we were all about to become unwitting cast members.

As I guided her into our famed Blue Lagoon room, meticulously designed to promote peace and tranquility with soundproof walls, an adjustable bed, and a calming spa tub—she immediately settled into the bed at a proud 45-degree angle, like a queen surveying her domain. "How do they look?" she asked me, craning her neck in a not-so-subtle attempt to steal a glance at her bandaged chest.

I did my best to assure her, “Everything looks good!” I said, hoping that would end the conversation. I handed her the standard ginger ale, saltines, and pain medication, expecting she’d be asleep soon. But within minutes, it became glaringly clear that Ms. Double Ds was not your typical drowsy post-op patient. Nope, she was one of those rare souls who react to pain meds like others do to three double espressos: instead of knocking her out, the meds had transformed her into a ball of boundless energy.

It had been an especially hectic day at the retreat. Every room had been turned over, a new round of clients had checked in, and the staff was on the brink of collapse from running around to ensure everything was flawless. By evening, most of the team had gone home, leaving Dale, our head chef, to clean up the kitchen and breathe a sigh of relief after the day's final dinner service.

Just as Dale was hanging up his apron, Ms. Double Ds sauntered into the kitchen like she owned the place, bandages her only attire. "So, what do you think of the 400s?" she asked with the gravity of someone asking about world peace. Dale, a culinary artist and not exactly a connoisseur of cosmetic surgery lingo, was utterly perplexed. “Uh... I think you made the right choice?” he said, hoping this was the correct answer.

Unfazed by his confusion, Ms. Double Ds launched into a mile-a-minute discourse about her surgery, the pros and cons of “400ccs” versus “450s,” and her life philosophy on implant size. She asked for a coffee, and Dale—our resident people-pleaser—obliged, though he wasn't sure caffeinating her further was advisable. But hey, what's a little more fuel to the already raging fire?

As she sat there in the dim kitchen lighting, shirtless and animated, Dale was trapped. He didn't dare leave her alone but couldn't quite figure out what to do with himself, either. Suddenly, as if struck by divine revelation, she started to peel off her bandages. With a dramatic gesture, she cupped her new assets and said, “I think I should have gone with the 450s,” looking to Dale for his sage advice.

Dale, a professional in all things kitchen but hopelessly out of his depth here, simply nodded. "No, really, you made the right choice!" he said, probably for the fifth time. Just as he was about to break into a cold sweat, wondering when someone would rescue him, fate played its next card.

As if summoned by the chaos, our resident con artist (known affectionately around the retreat as Mr. Gucci, due to his penchant for flashy designer wear) entered the scene, drawn in by the kitchen lights and the prospect of company. He walked in on Ms. Double Ds mid-monologue, pausing only briefly to assess the shirtless situation before slipping comfortably into his default suave mode.

With an air of well-practiced cool, he strolled up and leaned against the counter. "400s, huh?" he said with all the charm of a late-night talk show host. "Solid choice. You know, there's an art to these things." Ms. Double Ds lit up, delighted by his enthusiasm.

Sensing an opportunity to ride the wave of Ms. Double Ds's high-energy vibe, Mr. Gucci requested a drink, preferably something strong. Poor Dale, desperately needing an exit strategy, quickly mentioned we don't keep alcohol on hand for recovery patients—this was a wellness retreat, after all, not a Vegas hotel. But he did offer some cooking sherry as a last resort.

"Perfect," said Mr. Gucci, who, by this point, was clearly enjoying the bizarre nature of the evening. He sipped the cooking sherry with the same air of sophistication he would give a glass of fine Scotch, and every now and then would add his two cents to Ms. Double Ds's conversation, all while stealing amused glances at Dale.

By now, I'd returned to the scene, shocked to find the retreat's kitchen looking like a cabaret. Ms. Double Ds, half-bandaged and bandage-free, alternated between lifting her "400s" and offering Mr. Gucci her thoughts on life, beauty, and self-worth.

I approached with all the poise of a hostage negotiator, gently suggesting that we move the party back to her room and switch to decaf. Ms. Double Ds finally looked at me, gave her 400s one last triumphant shake, and allowed herself to be led back to the Blue Lagoon room. Fortunately, her doctor had prescribed Ativan for potential post-surgical anxiety, and with some convincing, she took it. Soon enough, she started to mellow out, her eyelids drooping as the meds took effect.

The next morning, the retreat staff gathered around like witnesses to a natural disaster, sharing wide-eyed stories of the night's spectacle. Our task now was simple: who was going to drive Ms. Double Ds home?

The staff drew straws, a process accompanied by grimaces, groans, and fervent prayers to avoid pulling the shortest one. Dale, who was still visibly traumatized, made it clear that he would not be doing it, no matter the straw's length. When the lot fell to me, I gave a resigned sigh, fortified myself with a final cup of coffee, and steeled myself for the ride.

By the time I reached her room, Ms. Double Ds was already buzzing around, bright-eyed, and chattering at a mile a minute. It was hard to believe she'd been up half the night; she seemed more energized than ever. As we loaded into the car, her conversation flowed freely, ranging from fashion advice ("Big boobs are back in, honey!") to critiques on interior design and even an impromptu analysis of my driving skills.

Every few minutes, she'd pause to ask, "So, what do you think of the 400s?" It became a mantra, a question that needed neither answer nor elaboration. I would nod, give her a thumbs-up, and repeat my assurance that the 400s were indeed perfect.

Back at the retreat, Dale was mulling over his future. As he looked over the coffee machine that had brewed the now-infamous late-night fuel, he made a decision: it was time for a career pivot. His chef's apron had been his pride and joy, but after a night with Ms. Double Ds, he realized it might be time to hand over the kitchen responsibilities to someone else.

The rest of us, too, would forever remember the night Ms. Double Ds lit up our quiet little retreat, turning a simple recovery stay into a memory for the ages. Her impact was as profound as her personality—and yes, her 400s.

As I finally waved her off, I took a deep breath, thankful that our retreat had survived its most unforgettable guest. She had left in her wake a handful of wide-eyed staff, a new anecdote we'd tell for years, and a renewed commitment to discretion on caffeine allowances for all future guests.

The legend of Ms. Double Ds lives on at the retreat, immortalized in whispered tales, exaggerated retellings, and Dale's occasional shudder at the mention of cooking sherry. She was a force of nature who barreled through our lives, leaving us laughing, stunned, and possibly scarred—but most of all, reminded that no two clients are ever the same.

Our retreat remains a haven of healing and peace, but every so often, when the air is just right, someone might bring up that legendary night and the gleeful energy of the woman who redefined what it meant to 'recover' after a cosmetic upgrade.

7

Mr. Gucci

Mr. Gucci was a study in contradictions: a man so sleek he looked like he walked straight out of a luxury cologne ad, yet as down-to-earth as your friendly neighborhood barista. When he swept through our doors, he made it abundantly clear that he wasn't here to take in the Colorado landscape, but to endure a high-stakes surgical recovery that, if successful, would grant him the chiseled abs he clearly felt were a divine right.

We'd seen a lot by then. As the retreat grew, Dale and I had transformed our operation from an intimate mom-and-pop setup into something a bit more... deluxe. Dale was finally able to set aside his role as the all-around errand butler, a role he'd mastered with perhaps a little too much gusto. We partnered with local restaurants for fresh menu offerings instead of juggling all the cooking ourselves, and hired staff to help give our guests a level of service worthy of their expectations.

But Mr. Gucci was different. He was not a typical patient or even a typical guest; he was, shall we say, an experience. Upon picking him up at the airport, the presence of designer everything—the shades, the shoes, the Louis Vuitton luggage—told us everything we needed to know. He greeted us with a casual smile, one that implied we'd all known each other in a past life. His attitude was warm but somehow enigmatic, like a novel you just can't put down.

We drove him to the Eucalyptus Estate room, a tastefully "masculine" suite where the furnishings were rich, dark, and woody—where even the air felt sophisticated. Mr. Gucci took it all in with an appreciative nod, his gaze lingering on the details as if weighing their elegance against the places he'd been. His expectations were high, and though he didn't say it, the approval in his eyes was enough to make me breathe a little easier.

Once he was settled, the conversation turned, of course, to the surgery. "You really think it's worth it?" he asked, eyes narrowed as if assessing the surgeon's entire resume through me.

"Oh, definitely. You're looking at six-pack heaven." I leaned in with a wink. "Just prepare for a little... drainage. A lot of tight garments. The whole routine."

He listened, nodding along with an almost childlike curiosity, though I could tell he was already prepared to take whatever the procedure threw at him. To Mr. Gucci, anything that didn't kill you made you hotter. Still, by day two, he was introduced to the unglamorous side of recovery, and I'd catch him grimacing as he wrangled himself into the compression garment, muttering things that could blister paint.

"Is this thing supposed to strangle you, or am I just special?" he'd ask, always with a wry grin, his humor intact even while wrestling with fabric that could probably double as industrial-strength elastic. If he was irritated, he'd quickly bounce back with that easy charm, cracking jokes and handling the ordeal with a dignity I'd only seen in people whose wardrobes were similarly limited to designer labels.

* * *

Within a week, he was wandering around the retreat like he'd lived there for years, mingling with guests and staff alike, a man who was equal parts mysterious and likable. As the days passed, a faint aroma began to accompany him—let's just say it wasn't our signature lavender scent. Gucci had somehow secured himself a substantial stash of cannabis, a feat we never questioned but couldn't help but admire. There he was, reclining in our common areas, eyes half-lidded, looking as serene as a monk on retreat. When you walked into a room he was in, you'd get a waft of that unmistakable "Colorado perfume," and soon enough, it became a feature of his presence, like a cologne you started to associate with him.

Mr. Gucci was the picture of mellow elegance, cracking jokes and waxing poetic about life while leaning back in his chair, practically floating. "I know what you're thinking," he'd say with a knowing smile. "But trust me, it's medicinal."

I didn't have the heart to tell him that we weren't about to stop him anyway. Unlike alcohol, it didn't make our guests rowdy, and if anything, it only seemed to enhance his charm, which he proceeded to lay on thick. There was no topic he wouldn't tackle, from the politics of fast fashion to the philosophy of "designer as a lifestyle." At some point, he was in our common area giving advice on compression garment hacks to other guests—"It's all about strategic wriggling," he said, smirking as he demonstrated.

* * *

Eventually, things took a slightly more peculiar turn. Packages began arriving at the retreat addressed to names none of us recognized. "Oh, those are mine," Mr. Gucci would say casually, as if explaining something as mundane as a coffee order. Each parcel seemed to carry an alias, each stranger than the last, yet each one accepted by Gucci with the same faint smile. By now, we were used to his curious quirks, and the mail was just another charming oddity in a list that kept growing.

I remember once venturing to ask him, "So... all these names. Do they mean anything?"

He gave me a quick, amused look. "Maybe they're just different versions of me," he said with a shrug, like this answer explained everything.

As if he sensed our curiosity, Gucci occasionally dropped snippets of his past. We learned he was "between ventures" and had traveled extensively, though the specifics were always shrouded in mystery. It felt almost cinematic–here was this character out of a caper film, lounging in our retreat, quietly conducting what I can only describe as his "business," whatever that entailed.

* * *

Our camaraderie grew to the point where we started socializing outside the retreat. By this time, Gucci had become such a fixture that it felt only natural to bring him along for outings. We went to dinner with him several times, where he was as generous with his wallet as he was with his laughter, covering tabs and buying drinks for the table. One afternoon, we even took a day trip to see some of the sites of Colorado with a friend of mine. Gucci was in his element, treating everyone like old friends and even guiding us with a playlist of songs he deemed "perfect for the altitude."

The friend I'd brought along was equally captivated by his charisma. He had that uncanny ability to make people feel like they were in on some grand, exclusive joke. As we drove back, he promised to visit again sometime, though something in his tone made me doubt we'd ever actually see him after he checked out.

* * *

Our last evening with Gucci proved to be one of our most memorable. As he packed up his belongings, I walked by to see him with a table full of shampoo bottles. He was pouring small portions of ground, fragrant green herb into each one with the precision of a chemist. I leaned against the doorframe, watching in silent amusement as he worked.

"Care to share the master plan?" I asked.

He looked up with a grin, "Just a little something I like to call ingenuity," he said, holding up a bottle like a prized treasure. "Security checks are no match for this kind of genius."

I wasn't convinced, but it wasn't my role to question his methods. After all, the retreat wasn't exactly in the business of doling out life advice—especially not to men who clearly had it all figured out. When I pointed this out to him, he only shrugged and said, "Look, if I've learned anything, it's that there's always a workaround. You just have to find it."

* * *

After he'd packed, dined us, and doled out gifts like he was Santa in Chanel, he finally departed, leaving behind an atmosphere of charm and mystery. A month later, while idly skimming the news, I came across an article about a wanted con artist who looked uncannily like our Mr. Gucci, reportedly seen "taking up new ventures" in the Caribbean. It took me a moment to process, and I laughed until I nearly fell out of my chair. The universe has a way of keeping secrets, I suppose.

In the end, we were left with the memory of Mr. Gucci—whoever he might truly have been. He represented an intersection of worlds that wouldn't normally collide: his high-flying life of luxury and intrigue, and our quiet retreat nestled in the mountains. And though he might have been a man of many names, he was, for that time, simply Mr. Gucci to us, a friend, a guest, and an unforgettable character who wandered into our lives with as much mystery as he left.

8

The Mafia Baby

Now that you have heard of so many of our colorful clients; let me introduce you to one of the younger ones. Just about 25 years old, straight out of Chicago, the kind of guy you'd expect to see in a black leather jacket and shades. We'll call him Anthony.

He looked every bit the Italian-American prince: slicked-back hair, gold chains gleaming, and a suit that might've been out of his dad's closet but was probably a gift from someone who owed him a favor. He stepped out of that limo like he owned the place, tossing a casual nod to the driver, who seemed to be trying to look invisible despite being in a bright red suit.

As Anthony swaggered through the door, I half-expected him to order a slice of pizza and start regaling us with his Chicago stories. Instead, his dad - yes, *the* dad, the voice on the other end of the phone who sounded like he might make cement shoes for a living – had pre-arranged everything. That voice! It was a thick Chicago Italian accent, gruff but polished, each word precisely enunciated as if the man's life depended on it. I half-expected him to sign off with, "You know who I am." He'd insisted we treat Anthony like gold, "Take care of my kid, capisce?" he'd growled over the phone. There was a sense of...let's call it "intensity" in his voice, the kind that made me wonder if we were about to perform surgery on the son of someone who could easily have been Tony Soprano.

Anthony, it seemed, had signed up for the deluxe "Waffle Iron Special" – our cheeky name for ab etching, where we'd carve him up to look like he'd just stepped out of a Men's Health cover shoot. All I could think was, *Maybe lay off the cannoli, kiddo.* He was on the chunkier side, and I couldn't help but feel that abs on him would be more like a garnish than a main course. But hey, business was business.

The night before his surgery, Anthony seemed totally chill. He hung out in his room, ordering room service like a king, binging some old mob movies, probably taking notes on how to look "tough" for when he got those chiselled abs. He was clearly enjoying his "vacation."

The day of the surgery, our team whisked him into the operating room at dawn. We anticipated a quick procedure. But a couple hours in, word came from the OR: Anthony's Waffle Iron Special had turned into the "Oops-We-Need-a-Tummy-Tuck Special." The doc had seen his "situation" and made the executive decision that a full-on tummy tuck was the only way to flatten that paunch. So now, instead of a discreet ab contour, Anthony was getting the full monty: hip-to-hip incision, aggressive lipo, new belly button. This was no six-pack; it was a renovation.

When they wheeled him back to his room, still loopy from the anesthesia, I thought, *This might not go over well with Tony Soprano Senior.* But little Anthony was blissfully out of it, so I let him sleep.

Several hours later, I knocked and walked in to check on him, expecting him to be groggy but fine. Instead, there he was, standing in front of the mirror, sobbing his heart out.

"Hey, Anthony, what's wrong?" I asked, trying to keep my voice calm.

He turned to me with wide, devastated eyes, pointing at the bandages peeking out from under his hospital gown. "What...what the *hell* is this?!"

I braced myself, taking a deep breath. *Here we go.* "So, um, the doctor decided that the Vaser lipo wasn't going to work, and he had to switch to a tummy tuck. That incision is just a necessary part of that procedure. You'll still look great, just, you know...a little different than you thought."

Anthony's face was a portrait of betrayal, as if I'd personally taken his six-pack dreams and thrown them out the window. "I was supposed to have abs, lady! Now I got a scar big enough for a shark attack story!"

"That's the spirit!" I tried to joke, regretting it the moment I saw his expression darken. *Note to self: don't suggest shark-attack origin stories to mobster offspring.*

From there, the tears just kept coming. Anthony's view of his future - and apparently his entire romantic life - had crashed and burned. He was convinced he'd never be able to take his shirt off at the beach, that no girl would ever look at him again. The drama was in full swing, and I had to hold back a sigh of resignation.

Over the next few days, the staff learned to steer clear. Some of the younger girls, bless them, had no patience for this level of sensitivity. They'd mutter things like, "Big baby," as they rolled their eyes and got back to their routines. One even whispered that he should be thrilled about losing his "super

G" (aka his gut). But me, I felt like someone had to look out for the guy. I'd check in on him and sit by his bedside, handing him tissues, telling him that the scar would fade and that girls cared more about his personality than a few marks.

"Look, kid," I'd say, trying to be gentle, "you're still the same Anthony. Girls are gonna love you - maybe even more because you've got a story now, right? This scar, it's like a...a battle wound."

"Yeah, but I didn't wanna be in the battle!" he'd shoot back, the tears returning, and I'd sit there, squeezing his shoulder, realizing this was going to take some time.

And it did. For days, he oscillated between panic attacks about his future love life and full Guido mode whenever his dad or friends called. "Ay yo, yeah, I'm doin' just fine! Jus' chillin' out here, livin' the life," he'd say, switching instantly from tear-streaked mess to suave, too-cool-for-words gangster. When the calls ended, the act dropped, and he was back to his sad monologues about his doomed beach life.

Finally, a week later, it was time for him to go home. He'd had time to process it, even if only slightly, and I was ready to see him go. But then, around 11 p.m. on his last night, the call came. I heard that bell ring, and I just knew. We drew straws to see who would go in, and, lucky me, I lost.

I walked in to find him pacing the room, a full-blown panic attack in progress. "I can't fly home alone!" he exclaimed, eyes wide. "You gotta come with me, please. I'll pay. First-class, anything."

"Anthony, listen, I'd love to help, but I've got a retreat to run," I protested, but his pleas (and an ungodly offer of cash) wore me down.

And so, the next morning, there I was, sitting beside a 25-year-old mob kid in first-class, gripping his arm like I was his life coach, guiding him through breathing exercises mid-flight. I've never met a person with such a fear of flying who simultaneously thought he was the toughest guy in the room. The flight was only four hours, but it felt like a lifetime. He was sweating, shifting, talking non-stop about all the things he could never do now because of his scar.

Finally, we landed in Chicago, and as I walked him through the airport, I was half-hoping to see Tony Soprano Sr. waiting with a cigar and a "Welcome home, son." Instead, we stepped outside to find an entourage: five black Escalades, parked like they were in formation. One by one, big, suited men stepped out, all of them looking like they meant business.

A tall, slick-haired man in a leather coat nodded at me before walking up to Anthony and giving him some kind of complicated secret handshake. They loaded him up, and off they sped without so much as a thank-you nod in my direction.

As I watched them drive off, I couldn't help but feel a little sad. The kid was going home, but he wasn't walking away unscarred - physically or mentally. I hoped, in some small way, that his scar would fade, not just for his own peace of mind but because he was so young, too young to let a few marks dictate his self-worth.

Then, I headed straight to a nearby diner, ordered myself a slice of Chicago's finest deep-dish pizza, and raised a glass of wine to surviving the week of a lifetime. As I waited to catch my flight back, I couldn't help but laugh, wondering how in the world I'd tell this story to the rest of the staff back at the retreat.

9

The Stripper

This was quite the patient. She arrived fresh from surgery—brand new breast implants and a butt lift, courtesy of one of our biggest supporters. The surgeon who had worked his magic on her had become a regular collaborator with our retreat. He loved sending patients to stay with us for at least a night, adding our recovery fees directly into his quotes so they didn't think twice about it. Normally, his office would cut us a check. But with this patient? Well, we got something a little more... unique. His nurse handed over a thick envelope, practically bursting with cash—mostly $1 and $5 bills. She shrugged and gave us a wink. "It's just part of her profession."

I raised an eyebrow, immediately guessing what kind of profession might involve a steady supply of low-denomination bills. Judging by the enhancements she'd just signed up for, I was willing to bet my next paycheck she was an exotic dancer.

Strippers take their craft seriously, I suppose. Upping her game with new curves was, apparently, all part of the job.

When she stepped into our retreat, she was everything you'd expect. Long, fluorescent yellow nails glistened as she held her purse, her hair a perfect weave with bright pink strands woven through it, and lashes so thick they practically cast shadows. She introduced herself with a name that was definitely *stage-worthy*, but for the sake of confidentiality, let's just call her *Aurora*. It seemed fitting. Like a rare, colorful phenomenon that appears suddenly and leaves an impression you don't forget.

We showed her to the Lavender and Lily Room, one of our favorites. She was immediately at home, though her confidence was impossible to miss. Aurora had that diva vibe, commanding attention and expecting things to go exactly her way. I had a hunch she'd be the star guest of the week.

Later that evening, things got even more interesting. Aurora's husband showed up to visit—and he was just as much of a character. There was a huge gold chain glinting against a baggy T-shirt, a couple of gold teeth flashing as he grinned, and a swagger that would make a mob boss envious. But it wasn't just him; he'd brought the kids, too. A lively two-year-old and a baby in a stroller, all piling into our quiet little recovery retreat like it was a family reunion. I couldn't help but smile. This diva had a real life outside of the stage lights, complete with kids and a devoted, if flashy, husband.

They'd come prepared, too—he'd swung by Burger King on the way over. Soon enough, the kids were happily munching on fries in the middle of the bed while Aurora and her husband shared a Whopper like it was date night. I brought her a ginger ale and some crackers, thinking the post-op meds might not mix well with greasy fast food, but she waved them off with a perfectly manicured hand, focused entirely on her burger.

After the kids had their fill of fries, her husband gathered them up and headed out, leaving Aurora to settle in for the night. She cranked up the TV volume and let out a laugh so loud it echoed down the hallway. I briefly considered asking her to keep it down, but something told me this diva was going to have things her way, and who was I to stand in her way?

The next morning, our recovery assistant, Courtney, checked on Aurora and helped her out of bed. She got her settled into one of our zero-gravity chairs, which we use to keep patients in the ideal healing position. Of course, Aurora had her own ideas about the best spot and positioned the chair right next to our prized Lily painting. I held my breath, thinking about how much we'd already spent cleaning that piece after past mishaps. Aurora, blissfully unaware, reclined in the chair, ready for her breakfast.

We offered her one of our famous smoothies—vanilla almond milk, frozen berries, and 30 grams of protein to jumpstart healing. Aurora accepted it, nestling in with her smoothie and morning meds, all set for a peaceful morning. Courtney checked in on her every so often until it was time for her to get ready to check out.

Then came the sound—a huge, echoing *thud.* All three of us rushed upstairs, bracing for what we'd find. There was Aurora, sandwiched between the floor and the zero-gravity chair, which had somehow tipped over backward. And if that wasn't dramatic enough, her strawberry smoothie had gone flying in the fall, splattering right onto the lily painting in bright pink streaks.

Courtney, Dale, and I stood there in stunned silence, taking in the sight. The smoothie looked like it had been launched out of a cannon, turning our cherished artwork into a chaotic splash of pink.

We all had our first instincts. Mine, honestly, was to rush to the painting and clean up the mess before the berry stains set in. But, doing the right thing, I scooped up Aurora from the floor, checking to make sure she was okay. Dale and Courtney scrambled to save the painting, dabbing away at the smoothie splatters with tissues and cloths, murmuring desperate prayers that they could salvage it yet again. Miraculously, they managed to wipe it down enough to avoid permanent damage, sparing us from yet another hefty bill. I breathed a sigh of relief. We still weren't in a position to be replacing $40,000 paintings.

Aurora, however, seemed completely unfazed. After we helped her back into the chair and cleaned up the smoothie mess, she acted like it was all in a day's work. With a graceful flick of her yellow nails, she gave me a look that practically screamed *What's the big deal?*

We got her cleaned up and dressed just in time, because her husband pulled up outside, right on cue. This time, he arrived in a silver Hummer, blasting Tupac so loud the whole block could hear it. He honked once, then hollered for her to come on out—clearly, he wasn't planning on coming inside.

Aurora gave us a quick wave, grabbing the to-go bag we'd packed with healing snacks and another smoothie. Her husband helped her into the Hummer, his gold chains clinking as he lifted her carefully into the seat. The kids were in the back, happily munching on yet another round of fries.

With a roar of the engine, they sped off, leaving us standing there with the faint echo of Tupac and a lingering sense of disbelief.

After they left, I was trying to relax. Just when I thought the day couldn't get any stranger, Courtney came over to me, holding the envelope of cash with a bemused expression. She fanned out the dollar bills, grinning, "I don't know if this counts as high finance, but hey, a payment's a payment, right?"

We all burst out laughing, shaking our heads. For all the chaos, for all the mess, we were left with the most bizarre souvenir of all—a cash-stuffed envelope that told the story of a diva, her pink smoothie, and a family whose love language seemed to be loud, flashy, and very, very colorful.

As I leaned back in my office chair, I took a deep breath. Just another day in the life, right?

10

The Firefighter

The Monarch retreat was finally riding high. Our cozy rooms were filled, our guests looked well cared for, and the team had grown into a finely tuned machine. Hundreds of clients had walked through our doors, the majority for simple check-ups, a little tuck here or tweak there. Nothing too wild. We thought we'd seen it all—or at least enough to rest easy.

Then came *the* call: our latest arrival was a firefighter. Not just any firefighter, but one from Kansas City who was seeing our esteemed Dr. Waffle Iron. Now, it's not unusual for Dr. Waffle Iron to help with the more, let's say, aesthetic side of medicine, sculpting abs here or a little lift there. But this particular client had signed up for the full "sculpture package"—abs, biceps, quads, and even calves. Yes, *calves.*

When the day came for his arrival, he strode in like a Midwestern George Clooney—chin held high, strong brow, and muscles that you see on those professional bull rider types. With all that rugged charm, the entire staff did a little double take as he walked through the lobby, the nurses glancing at each other, mouthing "whoa." The front desk was suddenly jammed with three or four extra staffers, all quite eager to see if he needed any help with, well, anything at all. He seemed to have this powerful, silent "do I make you swoon?" energy, and boy, did it work.

Now, I'll admit, I had some questions. What on earth was a strapping firefighter like him doing spending thousands on *extra* muscles? Was he secretly body-doubling for the next superhero film? Was he a Kansas City superhero by night?

After some small talk (and a little prodding from our swooning staff), he finally shared his story. Apparently, he'd landed a gig in a firefighter calendar—the kind that typically features brawny guys in nothing but firefighter pants, strategically carrying hoses or smoldering in their suspenders. But landing a calendar slot had given him new ambitions. This wasn't just a calendar—it was *the* opportunity. Suddenly, local fame as Mr. August had him gunning for modeling gigs, but he'd been told he needed "a little more definition." You know, just a little more... everywhere.

Here he was, ready to take his physique to uncharted territory, aiming to ignite more than just fires in his hometown.

As he went in for his consultation with Dr. Waffle Iron, the staff gossiped in hushed voices, whispering their excitement over his heroic day job and his clear commitment to his newfound modeling career. One nurse, Sharon, whispered, "I'm just saying, if that firefighter calendar needs a first responder nurse, I *am* CPR-certified." Another sighed, "I could carry him out of a fire. Or a moderately warm room."

The consultations flew by, and soon, our dear firefighter was prepped for the big day. To be fair, we'd never done this level of body sculpting before. Biceps, quads, calves—each one was a new frontier for our team, and we were all quietly wondering how he'd handle the whole ordeal. After all, most of our patients were just here for a little touch-up, not a muscle overhaul. But this was a man on a mission, and he was ready to go the distance.

As surgery day approached, the place was abuzz. The nurses were practically drawing straws over who would be assigned to his case. Our dear firefighter was the topic of every break-room chat, each nurse describing how stoic and polite he'd been. His Midwestern charm won over every staff member he met, making them feel like he was just your average guy... well, your average guy who was about to undergo an entire sculpting session to look like he'd stepped out of a Renaissance statue exhibit.

* * *

Surgery day was quite an affair. We got him suited up, and before long, the "transformation" began. As he headed off to the operating room, he was humming a country tune, keeping calm in his easygoing Midwestern way. Once under general anesthesia, Dr. Waffle Iron went to work, skillfully lasering, tucking, and placing implants in areas where Mother Nature had apparently left a bit of "definition" to be desired. Small implants were placed over his biceps—like mini bicep lifts—and, yes, even his calves got a little boost, to give them just the right amount of shape.

By the end of it, he looked... spectacular. Not to sound unprofessional, but there was something majestic about seeing this fellow morph into a living, breathing sculpture. His abs looked like they'd been hand-painted, his arms could have been on a Michelangelo, and those quads? They were things of beauty. The nurses were practically fanning themselves.

After the initial "unveiling" and his post-op care, he was given the infamous full-body compression suit—a piece of modern medical fashion that resembled a spandex masterpiece. It started at his wrists, hugged every inch of his torso, wrapped his quads, and only released its grasp around his ankles. With the gleaming black fabric and tight fit, he looked like a superhero or perhaps the newest member of a professional dance troupe.

The suit wasn't glamorous, but he wore it with the same charm and dignity he'd brought to everything else. He looked a bit like he was wearing one of those superhero costumes where every muscle is accentuated (but this time, the muscles were *real*). But bless him, he never complained, not even once. He'd shuffle down the hallway like a muscled Michelin Man, his face set in that familiar Midwestern calm.

* * *

As he settled into his week-long recovery, his polite demeanor continued to win over everyone. He could've been boastful or brash, but instead, he remained his humble, easy-going self. And so the young staff began to compete for "firefighter duty"—each nurse vying for a spot on his post-surgery care team, as though his mere presence was somehow medicinal.

Every morning, as the staff would take turns checking his vitals, they'd pepper him with questions. "Do you really fight fires?" one nurse asked, eyes wide. "Like, real fires?" His response was always modest, "Yes, ma'am, I do. And they get real hot."

He kept in touch with us after he left, sending a few modest updates on his "modeling career." He'd landed a couple of small gigs, a local ad here and there, and even a TV commercial for protein shakes. Turns out, his calendar gambit had paid off, and he was moving on to bigger things.

We often joked, long after he left, about what might have happened had he returned. Maybe he'd come back for a little chest boost next, or perhaps a dab of definition on his shoulders? Plastic surgery can be a bit like that, once you start, it's hard to stop. We half-expected him to drop us a line one day asking about "pec implants" or maybe just a full-body contour. But he never did. I guess he found what he was looking for in that one week with us, his muscles sculpted, his body a canvas transformed.

Looking back, that week with our Midwestern firefighter remains one of my fondest memories of the retreat. He arrived all tough-guy swagger, Kansas drawl, and muscular bravado, only to reveal a gentle, unassuming nature that charmed us all. And yes, his modeling career might've sparked with a firefighter calendar, but he ended up leaving a lasting impression on everyone here.

Because sometimes, it's the tough guys with a surprising sensitive side that remind you why you started this work in the first place. Whether for chiseling abs or mending hearts, the journey is always full of surprises. And every once in a while, those surprises come wrapped in a full-body compression suit with a dazzling smile and dreams big enough to keep the fires burning in Kansas City and beyond.

11

The Actress

It was a normal Tuesday morning at the Monarch Retreat when we received the call that would catapult our humble wellness haven into the limelight. The voice on the other end was unmistakably cool, even a bit dismissive, like they were phoning a pizza place instead of a high-end medical retreat.

"This is Dr. Beverly Hills," he said, and I swear I could hear him adjusting his sunglasses even over the phone. "We've got a VIP client for you. Very high profile. Think A-list."

A-list? The only "A-list" I'd ever encountered was the one I'd hastily written out on scratch paper before the holidays to remember family gift ideas.

Dale nearly spat out his coffee when I told him, his jaw dropping in the most comical way. I thought I'd need to scoop it off the floor. "This could put us on the map," he managed to say between shocked gulps of coffee. "I mean, beyond Denver."

We were suddenly reeling with excitement. Sure, Monarch Retreat had a good reputation among the locals and the occasional out-of-stater looking for a discreet recovery from a nip-and-tuck. But an *A-lister*? That was next level.

And then came the details. This famous actress—let's call her Ms. Star, as our nondisclosure agreements forbid me from even whispering her name—was flying in for a little "refreshing." Nothing too major, just a delicate bit of lipo and a subtle neck lift. Minor tweaks, but for someone who was known for their "natural beauty" and was the poster child for "aging gracefully," this was apparently akin to dismantling the Great Wall of China.

The paperwork arrived next. A mountain of contracts, NDAs, liability clauses, and confidentiality agreements, that stacked higher than the mile high city of Denver itself. We signed and signed, and Dale muttered, "I think they even have us swearing our future grandkids to secrecy."

They weren't taking any chances. We were essentially committing to an agreement that this actress would be, to us, like a ghost. Someone we'd never met, someone who had never been there. It was as if she were planning a high-stakes heist instead of a minor surgical recovery. But hey, the price was right—by "right" I mean mind-blowingly astronomical. The retreat was cleared, our staff was given a few days off, and only Dale and I were permitted to stay onsite. I explained to the staff that we were doing some "maintenance work" on the facilities. The maintenance work of not mentioning this celebrity's name ever again, as it turned out.

Finally, the big day arrived. Six black SUVs with tinted windows glided up our driveway, looking like a presidential motorcade. Out stepped Ms. Star, enveloped in a floor-length black cape and massive sunglasses that made her look more like an intergalactic sorceress than an actress. As she floated toward the Blue Lagoon suite, I swear I heard angelic choruses—okay, it might've been my imagination, but the whole scene was surreal.

She was followed by her entourage: six people in total, including her personal assistant (Ms. Bluetooth, we dubbed her, as her Bluetooth headset seemed welded to her ear), three towering bodyguards who looked like they could have been extras in a Marvel movie, a personal chef who, I learned, had a Master's in Gastronomy, and a... well, I never did figure out what the sixth person's role was. They could've been her aura consultant for all I knew. I half-expected to see them carrying a golden litter to transport her from one side of the suite to the other.

The entourage swept into the Blue Lagoon suite, which had a living area, kitchenette, and enough room to comfortably house a family of six. It was our most exclusive suite, and they moved in like they were planning to settle for the winter. Ms. Bluetooth was the first to speak to us, issuing commands as if she were the one in charge.

"Ms. Star prefers privacy, so all communication will go through me," she informed us in a tone that suggested I might be a minor inconvenience to the whole setup. "She will require hourly checks from her assistant—not you—just for post-op peace of mind. You may enter only if absolutely necessary. Understand?"

Dale and I exchanged a look, nodding obediently while trying to stifle laughter. Was this really happening? We were about to receive a small fortune to essentially be ignored and to have all communication relayed through Bluetooth Barbie.

As it turned out, Ms. Star was on an incredibly strict regimen. She was well-known for her "all-natural" lifestyle, a reputation carefully maintained over decades. The personal chef, Chef Obsidian—no joke, that's what they called him—brought in coolers full of her pre-prepared meals. "Each meal is exactly

275 calories," Chef Obsidian explained to me, eyes wide with the kind of dedication you'd expect from someone guarding the Holy Grail.

He handed over an index card listing each meal in agonizing detail: there were things like "hydrated chia pudding with a drizzle of organic Peruvian maca honey," and "raw kale salad with a mist of Tahitian sea salt." Apparently, not one molecule outside this dietary regimen was allowed to enter her body. I had to resist the urge to tell him that we also had a fantastic pizza joint that delivered to our doorstep.

We figured she was resting post-op and getting used to her new neck and jawline. Still, the only face-to-face encounter I had with her the whole night was when I was allowed in briefly for vitals. She lay there, fully reclined with the glasses still on, looking like some ethereal deity of Hollywood. Her entourage scurried about her like she was a newborn kitten.

The procedure had gone beautifully, but the atmosphere was tense. Ms. Bluetooth told me that Ms. Star needed the utmost peace and quiet, so all lights had to be dimmed, no sharp sounds, no talking above a whisper. It was more like preparing for a delicate art installation than hosting a recovering surgery patient. I was beginning to wonder if the next request would be to place rose petals in her footpath.

* * *

By nightfall, the quiet was almost eerie. Her entourage had set up camp in the adjoining lounge area. Her three bodyguards sat up, like sentinels, while her assistant checked her every hour on the dot. Meanwhile, Dale and I marveled at how easy this job was turning out to be. We were practically being paid to tiptoe.

But the real kicker was when they left. The following morning, Ms. Bluetooth instructed us that they'd be departing by noon. Ms. Star emerged from her suite, dressed, coiffed, and cloaked, without a single sign of the previous day's surgery visible. Her assistant led her through the lobby as her bodyguards cleared a path, not a hair out of place.

Before we knew it, the entourage was gone, leaving only a faint aura of high-maintenance energy and the distinct scent of sandalwood. It was as if a tornado had passed through the retreat and then politely cleaned up after itself.

* * *

With Ms. Star on her private jet back to L.A., it was now time for our own brush with fame: the *commercial.* As part of our deal with Ms. Star's team, we'd been connected with a media rep who was going to help us create an ad for Monarch Retreat. Local television only, but hey, we were about to be on the air!

The ad crew arrived that afternoon, hauling equipment that looked fit for a big-budget movie. They set up in our spa loft, with lighting, cameras, and a director who looked like he'd rather be anywhere else. He gestured us into place, talking in rapid-fire industry jargon, which only made Dale more jittery.

"Are we rolling yet?" Dale asked after the fifth take, sweating so much he practically needed his own makeup assistant. He was clearly not built for the spotlight, poor guy. Meanwhile, I was in my element. I smiled into the camera, relaying our story, the features of the retreat, and our high standards. I may have laid it on a little thick, but hey, this was my big moment!

After what felt like a hundred takes, we finally wrapped up. The crew assured us they'd edit the footage into something "perfect for our image." I had visions of the commercial playing during prime time, of calls flooding in, of our retreat being booked solid for months on end.

The ad aired precisely once. At 6 a.m. On a Tuesday. And never again. The phones stayed quiet, and Dale got to avoid another anxiety attack.

* * *

For weeks after, Dale and I kept laughing about our encounter with Ms. Star and her over-the-top entourage. If that's what fame meant, maybe being small-town famous wasn't so bad after all. Our commercial may not have made us Hollywood legends, but we were officially a little less unknown. And the actress? Well, she continued her "all-natural" lifestyle, her face and neck as refreshed as ever. Maybe, in some way, we'd given her the secret boost she needed to keep her legend intact.

Our first celebrity encounter may not have made us rich or famous, but it sure gave us a story we'd never forget. And who knows? Maybe someday we'll get another call from Dr. Beverly Hills.

12

Monarch 2.0

After just three whirlwind years, it became glaringly obvious that our beloved retreat was bursting at the seams. We needed more rooms, more space, and, honestly, a bit more sanity. Parting with the place felt like breaking up with a first love—bittersweet and full of "remember when" moments. This was the retreat where so many memories had been made: the impromptu staff dance-offs in the kitchen, the bizarre yet oddly effective ideas that somehow worked, and the clients who became like family. It was hard to imagine letting it go. For a brief, delusional moment, we thought, "What if we just keep this one and get a second place nearby?"

It seemed like a genius idea—on paper. The reality, though, was a different beast entirely. Managing two retreats while delivering the high-end, Dale-and-me-as-the-secret-sauce experience? Impossible. Unless cloning technology had miraculously advanced overnight, there was no way this was going to happen. We quickly realized that hiring a manager was out of the question too. Not because we didn't trust anyone, but because no sane person would willingly take on the chaos that we somehow thrived in. Let's be honest—Dale and I were basically duct tape holding the whole operation together, and you can't hire duct tape.

So, with a mix of excitement and trepidation, we began our search for a new place. This, of course, is where things went hilariously off the rails. We started looking at mansions in Cherry Creek. Mansions. Plural. Some with as many as 12 rooms. Twelve! Who even needs that many rooms? The mere thought of dusting them made me want to take a nap. We brought some of our staff along to tour these estates, creating a strange entourage that looked like we were filming the world's weirdest reality show. Some of the places were turnkey ready; others needed the kind of renovations that make you question every decision that led you to this point in life.

And then there was *that* house. Oh, *that* house. It was a beautiful property, but it was right next to a daycare center. Picture this: toddlers happily finger-painting and playing hopscotch on one side of the fence, while freshly stitched-up clients shuffled around like extras from *The Walking Dead* on the other. The juxtaposition was just too much. I could already hear the Yelp reviews: "My child has been having nightmares about zombies ever since ***they*** moved in." It was a hard pass.

But then, just when we thought we'd never find the right place, we stumbled upon what seemed like the perfect option. A brand-new construction with ten rooms, a prime location, and separate living quarters for Dale and me. Finally, a chance to have some semblance of personal space! We secured funding, met with the builder, and even started imagining how we'd decorate the place. It felt like a dream come true—until it didn't.

One day, in the middle of signing yet another stack of paperwork, I had a full-blown panic attack. I don't mean a little wave of anxiety; I mean the full chest-tightening, "I might die right here on this plush leather chair" kind of panic. As I gasped for breath, it hit me—an epiphany of sorts. We couldn't keep living *with* surgery patients. I mean, who willingly chooses that life? It was like signing up for a never-ending episode of *Grey's Anatomy*, except there was no McDreamy to distract us. If we went through with this, we'd be banishing ourselves to some kind of bizarre purgatory.

There'd be no escape, no normalcy. Just us, our clients, and their endless needs. The thought was terrifying.

That's when Plan B was born. We decided that instead of owning another retreat, we'd find a partner and rent rooms on an as-needed basis. It was genius, really. Why lock ourselves into one space when we could have flexibility? The search began anew, and this time, we cast a wider net. We met with posh hotels, chatted with apartment complexes willing to rent out entire floors, and even explored the possibility of partnering with high-end short-term rental properties.

Then, like a beacon of hope, we found it—a quaint boutique hotel in the heart of Cherry Creek. It was the kind of place where people went to sip high tea and pretend they weren't Googling how to pronounce "croissants." From the outside, it looked unassuming, but it had a stellar reputation for luxury and discretion. We were skeptical at first. Why would a place like this want to partner with us? But to our surprise, it was privately owned, and the live-in caretaker was open to the idea.

This caretaker, let me tell you, was a character straight out of a storybook. He was a towering six-foot-three with a jolly laugh that could shake the windows. Over a ridiculously fancy lunch, we pitched our idea. I could see Dale's eyes light up with a mix of Christmas-morning excitement and pure relief. I knew exactly what he was thinking: "If we move our retreat here, I'll never have to cook another meal or pick up takeout again." And honestly? I was thinking the same thing.

The hotel had everything we needed—private entrances for discreet client arrivals, a top-notch restaurant, and a stellar reputation. We even managed to broker a deal that allowed us to move in our luxury adjustable beds and swap out the modest TVs for our obnoxiously large ones. It was like winning the lottery.

With ten rooms ready to go and a small office for administration, we felt like we'd hit the jackpot. To top it off, one of our former clients, Paige, offered to join our team. Paige had spent a long, tear-filled week recovering at our retreat and had somehow become one of our biggest fans. When she offered to handle administrative tasks, we didn't hesitate. Who better to answer the phones and reassure clients than someone who could say, "I've been where you are"?

The move was equal parts chaos and excitement. There were adjustable beds to transport, TVs to install, and a thousand little details to sort out. But through it all, there was a sense of hope and possibility. This wasn't just a new chapter; it was a chance to finally create some balance in our lives. For the first time in years, it felt like we were stepping into something sustainable—something that could grow with us, rather than consume us.

As we planned for our grand opening, I couldn't help but marvel at how far we'd come. From our humble beginnings to this elegant boutique hotel, it had been a wild ride. And while the journey wasn't without its hiccups, I wouldn't trade it for anything. Well, except maybe a lifetime supply of high tea and scones.

13

The Rag Doll

The grand opening of our new retreat was nothing short of spectacular. We weren't just celebrating; we were basking in the glow of our hard-earned success. After three years of relentless work and achieving a coveted five-star rating, we finally felt like the "it" place for post-op recovery. Surgeons from Denver, their staff, and even some from outside our usual circles attended. A couple of them even mentioned seeing our commercial—imagine that! But mostly, it was word-of-mouth magic that brought everyone in.

Even the hotel staff joined in. The kitchen and housekeeping crews were particularly intrigued, as if waiting for a parade of eccentric clients who might rival the bizarre episodes of a reality TV show. Some probably wondered if they should start updating their résumés, anticipating scenes too wild for their nerves.

And then, we met her. Our very first client after the grand opening—**Ms. Raggedy Ann**, as she came to be affectionately known—made an impression that still has us laughing (and cringing) to this day.

* * *

If you've read this far, you've likely heard of Dr. Waffle Iron, the king of chaos and chiseled abs. But let me introduce you to another surgical artist we'll call **The Doll Maker.** His specialty? Full head-to-toe body lifts for people who've lost an astounding amount of weight. This isn't your typical nip-and-tuck; this is an epic transformation that makes Frankenstein's stitching look like amateur hour. Stitches started at the feet, zigzagging up thighs, across the stomach, down arms, and even into the armpits. It was surgery on a level that inspired awe—and a bit of terror.

When the Doll Maker's office called us about accommodating one of his patients, we were thrilled... until we heard the details. This wasn't going to be a simple pick-up.

No, this was a **10-hour surgery**, with a patient requiring IV fluids, oxygen, and possibly divine intervention. I briefly considered investing in a stretcher, an ambulance, and a full medical team. Instead, we had our trusty Jaguar and sheer determination.

* * *

Dale and I geared up for the evening pick-up, which already felt doomed to chaos. The Doll Maker's team mentioned six drains, extra IV bags, and antibiotics, delivered in the same casual tone one might use to describe their morning coffee order. By the time we arrived, it was nearly 8 PM, our latest pick-up ever—outside of that infamous Dark and Stormy night with "Frank" that you may remember reading about earlier on.

When we entered the surgical suite, I was speechless. The patient—Ms. Raggedy Ann—was more stitches than skin, swathed in drains resembling tiny grenades filled with blood. She was so out of it from anesthesia that she could barely hold her head up. And the pièce de résistance? They handed me a list of post-op instructions that read like the manual for assembling a spaceship. Oh, and did I mention they expected her to fit in a Jaguar?

* * *

Dale's face was priceless when he saw her being wheeled out, oxygen tank dragging behind and IV bags swaying. His eyes nearly popped out of his head as he muttered, "Are we sure we aren't kidnapping someone?"

Together, we heaved Ms. Raggedy Ann into the car. The dry-cleaning hook in the Jaguar became an impromptu IV pole, and the oxygen tank rolled around in the backseat like a rogue missile. I silently prayed the police wouldn't pull us over, imagining their faces as they peeked inside: "Ma'am, is this a crime scene or a science experiment?"

* * *

By some miracle, we made it back without a hitch. Thankfully, the retreat had a private entrance and elevator, sparing the hotel guests from what would have been the most horrifying episode of *Nip Tuck they have ever seen.* But as fate would have it, the elevator ride didn't go unnoticed. One of the young room service attendants caught sight of us wheeling Ms. Raggedy Ann out. His jaw dropped as he stared at the patchwork of stitches and drains.

I could almost see the thought bubble over his head: **"What in the name of hospitality is going on here?"**

* * *

Settling Ms. Raggedy Ann into her room felt like preparing for an overnight ICU shift. We checked her oxygen levels, monitored fluids, and stayed religiously on top of her pain meds. My ICU trauma nurse instincts kicked in, but I couldn't help but think: **"This is not what we meant by a luxury retreat."**

To her credit, Ms. Raggedy Ann didn't make a peep of complaint. By 4 AM, she was awake and cheerful, despite looking like the world's most extreme game of Operation. She even chatted about her incredible journey–losing 200 pounds and finally completing her transformation. Her resilience was inspiring... if not slightly baffling.

* * *

By 10 AM, she was walking around her room like nothing had happened. Meanwhile, I was contemplating whether to add "amateur EMT and paramedic" to my résumé. The staff and I were equal parts relieved and traumatized. While we were thrilled to have successfully managed her care, none of us were eager to see another case like this anytime soon.

Lessons Learned

The experience left us with a few takeaways:

1. **We might need to charge extra for Raggedy Ann-level cases.**
2. **The Jaguar can double as an ambulance... but maybe invest in plastic seat covers.**
3. **Hotel staff will never look at us the same way again.**
4. **The Doll Maker might be a genius, but his patients should come with a warning label.**

In hindsight, it was a hilarious, heart-pounding adventure that added to the ever-growing list of reasons why our retreat is unlike any other. And while I wouldn't wish another Raggedy Ann situation on anyone, it sure makes for a story worth telling over coffee—though maybe not over breakfast.

14

The UFC Fighter

It's not every day that celebrities walk into your life, but with Dr. Waffle Irons' reputation for crafting abs so sharp they could julienne a carrot, we were getting used to it. Still, when we got the call about a world-famous UFC fighter from London booking with us, it added a little extra buzz to the clinic.

This wasn't just any fighter. The man had a record so impressive that even Dale, our resident "sports encyclopedia" and part-time coffee spillage expert, got starry-eyed. As for me, well, my knowledge of UFC extended to knowing it involved a lot of blood, sweaty men, and commentators shouting things like "He's going for the armbar!" But I was intrigued.

The moment our client [with a keen resemblance to Jason Statham] walked in, it was like a scene from a Guy Ritchie movie. He had the swagger, the accent, and a skintight white tee that left absolutely no mystery about his muscle definition. Seriously, you could probably use his biceps as a topographical map. Naturally, we had all Googled him ahead of time. His record was stellar: nine wins in his last ten fights. But it was the Calvin Klein ads he hinted at during check-in that stole the show. He confessed he needed more than a six-pack—an eight-pack, maybe even a ten-pack—because fame demands *extra abs.*

"Fame sure does have a price," I muttered to Dale as we watched our guest toss his luggage onto the concierge cart like it weighed nothing. Dale, of course, was too busy grinning like a kid in a candy store.

Now, if there's one thing we've learned about hosting high-profile clients, it's that they bring out the best—and the weirdest—in people. Staff members suddenly become "available" for every possible shift. People who usually complain about stocking towels are suddenly fighting over who gets to deliver an extra pillow. Even the hotel staff joined the chaos. Room service waitresses mysteriously started applying fresh lipstick before deliveries. Housekeeping practically set up camp outside his suite, whispering things like, “Do you think he’s awake yet?”

He certainly knew the effect he had on people. One afternoon, I walked into his suite with some post-op care instructions, only to find him in his Calvin Kleins (surprise, surprise), flexing in front of the mirror. “Just gotta appreciate the 'before' one last time,” he said with a wink. I resisted the urge to roll my eyes and instead handed him the paperwork. He didn’t notice; he was too busy giving his reflection a pep talk.

***

On surgery day, the entire clinic buzzed like a hive of caffeinated bees. Dr. Waffle Irons was, of course, calm and collected, the Michelangelo of abdominal artistry. The fighter, however, was surprisingly chatty. As the anesthesia took hold, he mumbled something about "landing that billboard over Big Ben." Ambitious, but okay.

The surgery was a smashing success. By the time Dr. Waffle Irons was done, this guy’s abs looked like they belonged on the cover of *Abs Monthly* (not a real magazine, but it should be). I'm not even sure how it's anatomically possible to have that much definition. Dale took one look at the post-op photos and whispered, "That's not an eight-pack. That's a masterpiece."

During his week-long stay, our fighter regaled us with tales of his UFC battles. Dale was glued to his side, practically drooling over stories about spinning kicks and last-minute knockouts. The rest of us, however, were just trying to maintain professionalism while he strutted around in his underwear every chance he got.

One afternoon, I caught him doing pushups. "Should you even be doing that yet?" I asked, genuinely concerned. "Can't let the new abs get lazy," he replied, flashing a grin that probably could've sold toothpaste.

It wasn't all flexing and storytelling, though. The man had charm. He knew the names of everyone on staff by the end of the second day and even offered a few UFC-style nicknames. I was "Boss Lady" (I'm still not sure if that's a compliment or a dig), and Dale became "Stats," which he wore like a badge of honor.

***

By the end of the week, the clinic felt like it had been hit by a reality TV show. The younger waitstaff were smitten, and one of them even slipped him her number. "In case you need... recommendations for sightseeing," she stammered. He tucked the note into his wallet with a grin. Fame, muscles, and a British accent—it's like the man was engineered in a lab for maximum swoon effect.

Before he left, he made us all promise to stay in touch. "If you're ever in London, I'll sort you out with tickets to a fight," he said. "And I'll send you an autographed copy of the Calvin Klein ad when it's out." We waved him off at the airport, Dale practically bouncing with excitement.

Weeks passed, and life at the retreat returned to its normal rhythm. Dale checked the mail religiously, hoping for that autographed ad. It never came. But one day, while scrolling through social media, I stumbled upon a photo: a massive Calvin Klein billboard in the heart of London. And there he was, abs gleaming under the city lights.

I showed Dale the photo. "Guess he landed the ad," I said. Dale nodded, grinning. "We helped make those abs famous," he said, his voice full of pride.

Fame might have a price, but sometimes, it's worth it for the laughs and the stories we get to keep.

15

The Oil Tycoon

When our retreat intake coordinator warned us about our next VIP guest, we were bracing for trouble. The words *"high maintenance"* and *"wealthy oil tycoon"* set the tone for what would undoubtedly be an unforgettable experience. And sure enough, when his six-figure pickup truck rumbled into the lot, we realized we were in for something extraordinary.

The man who stepped out was a walking Texan stereotype: tall, tan, and rocking a cowboy hat so wide it probably needed its own zip code. His voice, like his personality, was larger than life, booming loud enough to rattle windows. Four pieces of designer luggage tumbled out of the truck bed, each more excessive than the last. It wasn't long before we realized the *oil tycoon* came with his own set of quirks—and we were about to meet every one of them.

As part of our white-glove service, we assisted clients with unpacking their bags. That's when I made the first discovery: an entire suitcase dedicated to *man makeup.* Foundation, concealer, brow pencils–the works. His collection could rival a beauty influencer's haul.

I didn't ask questions, but after sneaking a closer look at his face, it all made sense. His skin was smooth and flawless, like a porcelain doll with a Southern drawl.

The oil tycoon wasn't shy about his beauty regimen either. "Gotta look my best," he said with a wink, adjusting his hat and flashing a dazzlingly white smile. He'd come for a facelift and eyelid lift, determined to knock a decade off his appearance, and with a fortune at his disposal, he was ready to pay for perfection.

The surgery went smoothly, courtesy of our two younger, dashing surgeons, whom we haven't yet spoken about but have worked with often. They were known for their "mommy makeovers," and their clients were often uneventful and "in and out" of our retreat without any drama. This oil tycoon was no mommy, of course. He was, however, a man of precision and flair, and he was already thrilled with the results by the time we wheeled him back into his suite.

It seemed like his recovery would be uneventful. But by evening, the call bell rang.

* * *

Bridgette, our bright-eyed nursing assistant and a mere 20 years old, was the first to respond. Moments later, she returned to the office looking pale.

"What happened?" I asked.

"He needs help... with his *weights,*" she whispered.

"Weights? Like dumbbells?"

She shook her head furiously. "No. For his... um, *penis pump.*"

I stared at her, stunned. "His *what*?"

Apparently, our oil tycoon had recently undergone another procedure involving a very specialized enhancement device. Post-surgery, it required attaching weights to "strengthen" things. None of us had been informed, and poor Bridgette had just walked into a situation that could scar most nursing students for life.

Despite her horror, Bridgette had handled it like a champ. She didn't assist with the *dangling* part, of course—just helped organize his setup. Still, I couldn't shake the mental image as I went to talk to him.

"Sir," I said diplomatically, "maybe hold off on the weight exercises until tomorrow. You've just had surgery, and the anesthesia and pain meds might make things... unsteady."

"Good point!" he boomed. "Don't wanna fall over in the buff with my rig hangin' out!"

I nodded gravely, though I nearly bit my tongue trying not to laugh.

***

The next morning, I caught him nicotine gum like a teenager in study hall.

"Sir, you know you can't have nicotine," I said, trying to keep my tone light.

"It's not smoking!" he protested. "I quit cigarettes, docs orders!"

"Yes, but the *nicotine* itself slows healing. It constricts blood vessels."

Without a word, he spat the gum out—straight into my hand. I froze, staring at the wad of sticky nicotine-coated gum now nestled in my palm.

"Well," I muttered, "I guess that's one way to quit."

Despite the unusual start, the oil tycoon turned out to be a surprisingly likable guy. He regaled us with stories of his sprawling ranch, jet-setting lifestyle, and how he struck it rich in the oil business. His booming laugh echoed through the halls, turning what could've been an awkward recovery into a comedy show.

He even shared tidbits of his personal life: his late wife, his love of golf, and the joy of spoiling his grandkids. But nothing beat the casual way he'd toss out phrases like, "And that's how I ended up meeting the President" or "So there I was, eating caviar on a yacht in Monaco..."

By the end of his stay, we weren't just his caretakers—we were his audience.

* * *

When the week ended, the oil tycoon packed up his designer luggage, carefully applied his man makeup, and thanked us with his signature booming laugh. But before he left, he made us an offer we couldn't refuse.

"Y'all ever been to Texas?" he asked.

We shook our heads.

"Well, come on down to my ranch! All expenses paid. You'll love it—guest house, golf course, spa, the works."

We thought he was joking. He wasn't.

* * *

A month later, Dale, Bridgette, Courtney, and I found ourselves on a plane to Texas. His ranch was exactly as grand as he'd described: a guest house bigger than most mansions, a private golf course, and a spa that rivaled any luxury retreat.

He joined us for a few rounds of golf, sharing even more outrageous stories and insisting we try every amenity his ranch had to offer. The highlight, however, was the tour of his main house, a sprawling estate covered in photos of him shaking hands with celebrities and politicians.

For all his wealth and bravado, the oil tycoon seemed genuinely thrilled to have us there. It was clear that behind the makeup and the booming laugh was a man who valued connection—and wasn't afraid to share his good fortune.

We still hear from him occasionally—postcards from exotic locales, stories of his latest adventures. Every time, we laugh, remembering the man with the cowboy hat, the flawless complexion, and the unforgettable recovery routine.

He came to us for a facelift but left us with memories—and a story—bigger than Texas itself.

16

The Recluse

Some stories just have a way of sticking with you, don't they? And Roxanne's was one for the books. If you've ever doubted the resilience of the human spirit—or liver—then allow me to introduce you to a guest who redefined *both* while proving that even in chaos, kindness can shine through.

Roxanne first checked into our retreat a few years ago for a facelift, a procedure that quietly transformed her into a softer, more youthful version of herself. She barely spoke, rarely used the staff call bell, and left behind nothing but whispers about her beauty and a generous tip. On her second visit, she returned for a breast lift, equally understated and self-contained. If we had a "guest hall of fame," she'd have been a shoo-in for "Most Low Maintenance."

By her third visit, Roxanne's familiarity with Monarch Retreat made her bold enough to opt for our newest offering: the full monty package. This wasn't just your run-of-the-mill recovery. It included everything from early check-ins at our standard hotel rate with a slight markup for transportation to a bespoke healing regimen featuring staff check-ins, nutritional guidance, and round-the-clock pampering. She booked three full weeks, paying a small fortune for two weeks of top-tier post-op care.

This time, Roxanne was here for a neck lift and a revision of her breast lift—apparently, the original wasn't up to her standards. At just 5'4" and 105 pounds, she was a tiny but formidable force. She drove herself all the way from Arizona with a cooler in tow, her petite frame somehow balancing her soft-spoken demeanor and her resolve for perfection.

* * *

When Roxanne arrived, we reminded her of our fully stocked menu and room service options. She politely dismissed the offer, insisting that she only ate certain foods and needed to stock up herself. Her return from a grocery run was notable—not because of the organic produce or artisanal snacks we expected, but because her cooler was packed with two enormous jugs of vodka.

Now, we weren't alarmed at first. People are quirky, and maybe she just liked a little nip of something strong to celebrate her future flawless neck. Surgery day arrived without incident, and Roxanne, ever the trooper, handled the neck lift and breast revision like a pro. Her surgeon, known for neck lifts so tight they practically redefined swallowing mechanics, delivered results that were both precise and impressive.

Settled back into her room with ice packs and pain meds, Roxanne remained her usual quiet self. She didn't call for assistance unless absolutely necessary, so we made it a point to check on her every four hours.

The morning after surgery, our night staff casually mentioned peeking into Roxanne's cooler to grab her a snack. It wasn't hummus or yogurt they found—it was the vodka, two gallons of it, sitting unapologetically next to a bag of celery sticks. Still, we gave her the benefit of the doubt. Perhaps the vodka was meant for later or was a quirky gift for someone back home.

But as the days unfolded, it became clear that Roxanne wasn't saving the booze. She was consuming it.

The first sign was her emotional outbursts. She hated her results—her neck, her breasts, her everything. She announced her intent to "do it all over again" and booked consultations for more surgeries before the stitches from her current procedures had even healed. Her fixation on "fixing" herself hinted at something deeper, and we began to worry.

***

The floodgates opened a few days later: her husband, the faceless financier behind her procedures, was leaving her for a younger woman. Suddenly, her relentless pursuit of perfection made sense. She was scrambling to compete with time, youth, and her husband's wandering eye. It wasn't just surgery she was after—it was validation.

We did what we could to comfort her. The staff made frequent visits to her room, sitting with her in the dark. She never watched TV or engaged with anything outside of her own thoughts. Her grief was palpable, and we began to see the real Roxanne—not the polished, quiet guest but a woman grappling with heartbreak and an overwhelming sense of inadequacy.

As her emotional state worsened, her drinking increased. The room, once pristine, began to resemble a frat house after homecoming weekend. Lamps were overturned, food was scattered across the floor, and the faint smell of spilled vodka hung in the air.

The housekeeping staff, who had seen everything from spilled coffee to spilled secrets, began asking if we'd expanded into psychiatric care. We weren't therapists, but we were human. While we couldn't stage an intervention, we gently encouraged Roxanne to cut back. We reminded her that alcohol slows healing, that she was beautiful as she was, and that any man would be lucky to have her. She nodded politely but seemed impervious to our reassurances.

***

Determined to "fix" herself, Roxanne scheduled consultations for additional procedures, including a vaginoplasty. Yes, she wanted to tighten even the most private of regions, as though her self-worth was tied to every inch of her body.

By now, her surgeon had discontinued her pain medications, citing concerns about her drinking. Roxanne, unbothered, continued her vodka routine. She oscillated between depression and manic energy, and we began to suspect she might be dealing with bipolar disorder. But what could we do? She was an adult, and while we could advise her, we couldn't make decisions for her.

The climax of Roxanne's saga arrived in the form of a phone call. Her husband, no longer content to be a silent benefactor, exploded into our office with the fury of a man whose credit card bill had finally tipped him over the edge.

"What the hell is a Monarch Retreat?" he yelled.

Dale, our unflappable receptionist, calmly explained our services.

"Well, whatever it is, Roxanne is trying to bankrupt me!" the husband roared. He canceled his card on the spot and demanded we check her out immediately.

Roxanne's reaction was classic Roxanne. She shrugged, muttered something about how "it's been fun," and packed her belongings without a hint of drama. At checkout, she signed her bill and added a generous tip—likely as one final jab at her soon-to-be ex-husband.

And just like that, she was gone. For nearly two months, she'd been a fixture at Monarch Retreat, a walking contradiction of elegance and chaos. We never heard from her again, but she left a lasting impression.

Roxanne was more than just a guest. She was a reminder that behind every glamorous exterior lies a complex human being with fears, insecurities, and struggles. Despite her flaws—and there were many—she was kind, sweet, and deeply human.

We often joked about writing a book about our guests, but Roxanne's story would undoubtedly deserve its own chapter. From her vodka-stocked cooler to her emotional breakdowns, she taught us lessons about resilience, heartbreak, and the lengths people go to feel worthy.

Wherever she is now, we hope Roxanne found peace. And if she didn't, we hope she at least switched to something less harsh than vodka. Cheers, Roxanne—you'll always be remembered.

17

Room 403

There's a universal truth in post-op care: no amount of medical training prepares you for *people.* Swelling? Bruising? Sure, we're experts. But dealing with a human tornado in silk scarves and a bedazzled neck brace? That's an elective no one offers in nursing school. The story I am about to tell you has a high potential to fill a horror anthology, and is definitely at the top of the "Please-God-Let-Me-Forget-This" list. Room 403. What started as a regular post-surgery recovery turned into a tale so infamous that even the hotel staff would later ask us, with wide eyes and bated breath, "It's not another 403, is it?"

It began innocently enough—or as innocently as anything involving a facelift, lasers, and a questionable plastic surgeon can. The guest in question was an heiress. Not just any heiress, mind you, but the daughter of a famous inventor whose identity we were too polite (read: too terrified) to ask about. Rumors swirled. Did her father invent the electric toothbrush? The retractable dog leash? A silent jet engine? No one knew, and honestly, no one cared. What mattered was that she had money, eccentricities, and a reservation with us after an appointment with the enigmatic "doll maker."

This wasn't your typical nip-and-tuck situation. We're talking about an eight-hour procedure involving a facelift and full laser resurfacing–basically, a "let's burn your skin off and hope for the best" approach. The name "doll maker" didn't exactly inspire confidence, but hey, the rich are weird.

***

Courtney and Dale were assigned the pickup. When a procedure was this extensive, we always sent two staff members. The heiress needed oxygen, IV support, and probably a small miracle to make it back in one piece.

When they returned to the garage that evening, I met them to help unload. I was immediately struck by the look on their faces. Courtney, usually chipper and chatty, was pale and silent. Dale, normally unshakable, looked like he'd just left a crime scene, the kind you might see on and episode of Law and Order.

"What happened?" I asked, my voice low.

Courtney just shook her head, her eyes wide. She tilted her head toward the back of the vehicle in a way that screamed *Don't make me say it.*

Bracing myself, I opened the door—and there she was.

The heiress was unconscious, thank God, or she might've been offended by the string of profanities that flew out of my mouth. Her face—oh, where to start? One eye was fully open, staring blankly in two directions at once, while the other had migrated halfway down her cheek. Her skin was shiny, raw, and coated in what looked like an inch-thick layer of petroleum jelly. She resembled a wax figure from a nightmare carnival.

"Is this... normal?" I whispered.

"Don't ask me," Dale muttered. "I just drive the jag."

"Well, it has to be swelling," I rationalized. "It *has* to be."

***

Room 403 was just another room—until that night. We wheeled her in, propped her up at a 90-degree angle, and started icing her face. The oozing began almost immediately. One of her displaced eyes was leaking a pale pink fluid that soaked tissues faster than we could replace them.

Bridgette, one of our braver staff members, took the first shift. "It's just a face," she joked nervously. "How bad can it be?"

She returned an hour later, her face as pale as a ghost. "I... I can't," she stammered. "It's like... she's melting."

We decided to rotate shifts to minimize psychological damage. Staff reactions ranged from stunned silence to whispered prayers. By some miracle, the heiress never asked for a mirror that night, sparing us from what would've surely been a scene worthy of Greek tragedy.

The next morning, we prepared for chaos. We were overbooked, with twelve patients in a facility meant for ten. The staff was stretched thin, flipping rooms and juggling post-op care. Bridgette, fortunately or unfortunately, was assigned Room 403 again.

"Just... try not to look directly at her face," I advised.

She nodded grimly and headed off with a breakfast tray. Minutes later, the scream came.

Not just any scream. The kind of scream that makes you drop whatever you're doing and assume the worst.

I sprinted down the hall, my heart pounding. Inside Room 403, I found Alice, one of the hotel's waitresses, frozen in place. The breakfast tray lay shattered on the floor, eggs and toast scattered everywhere.

The heiress was sitting up in bed, looking confused but otherwise unfazed. Alice, on the other hand, was on the verge of tears.

"I... I... I can't," she stuttered, backing away.

I quickly ushered Alice out of the room. "It's fine," I lied. "She's just... healing."

"THAT'S healing?!" Alice shrieked. "It looked like her face was sliding off!"

Alice clocked out immediately. I had to assure the hotel manager that we wouldn't subject their staff to another Room 403 ever again. Meanwhile, I returned to find Bridgette frantically trying to clean up the mess.

"She's asking for a mirror," Bridgette whispered.

I froze.

* * *

The moment we'd all dreaded had arrived. But what could I do? Denying her a mirror would only make her suspicious. This was definitely not a *'Mirror, Mirror, on the Wall'* moment for her.

Taking a deep breath, I fetched the largest mirror I could find and handed it to her.

She studied her reflection for an excruciatingly long moment.

"What do you think?" she finally asked. "Does everything look okay?"

I stared at her, utterly speechless. Did she not notice that one of her eyes was oozing blood and the other was playing hide-and-seek with her cheekbone?

"Well," I stammered, "I think you're just swollen right now. We'll see your surgeon tomorrow, and I'm sure everything will settle."

She nodded thoughtfully. "Good. I thought so."

Thought so? THOUGHT SO?! I wanted to scream, but instead, I excused myself and ran back to the staff office, where I promptly collapsed into a chair.

***

The next day, we took her to her follow-up appointment. The doll maker greeted us with the same unnerving calm he always had.

"Skin's healing nicely," he said, peering at her like she was a mildly interesting science experiment. "The eyes are just a little swollen. Keep icing."

A *little* swollen? The man had clearly lost all connection to reality.

We wheeled her back to the car, still trying to process what we'd witnessed. "Did he actually say 'nicely'?" Courtney asked.

"He did," I replied. "And I think we're all going to need therapy."

* * *

The heiress checked out the following morning, leaving behind a trail of bloody tissues, half-empty IV bags, and a staff with severe emotional scarring.

To this day, none of us know what became of her. Did her face ever heal? Did her eyes find their way home? Did the doll maker finally admit he was in over his head? We'll never know.

But Room 403? It became a legend. New staff were briefed on its history during orientation. The hotel manager started asking, "It's not another 403, is it?" every time we booked a room. And whenever someone complained about a tough shift, we'd remind them:

"At least it's not Room 403."

Room 403 became a symbol of survival. A test of strength. A badge of honor. And while none of us would wish that experience on anyone, it made for one hell of a story.

To this day, Room 403 remains a cautionary tale—a grim reminder of what happens when you mix vanity, experimental surgery, and just a touch of madness.

A Farewell and A New Beginning

It's funny how life has a way of making you look back at things and realize just how much you've endured and how far you've come—often in the blink of an eye. At The Monarch Retreat, we had reached the big milestone of caring for over 800 clients by the end of our fourth year. I don't know if that number is impressive or just a mirror to our utter lack of better judgment at the time, but either way, we were at a crossroad—again.

Now, I know the phrase "crossroad" is as overused as an office coffee machine that hasn't been cleaned in a decade, but in this case, it was fitting. You see, Dale and I were facing a decision that most business owners face at some point: should we expand, or should we throw in the towel?

We had been turning away guests left and right, not because we didn't want to help, but because we were so financially strapped by running The Monarch that we couldn't fit any more into our already bursting schedules. It was like trying to fit one more pair of shoes into a closet that was already packed to the brim—every time you think there's no more room, you find a way to stuff it in and hope for the best. Our expenses were mounting, we hadn't taken a single day off (not one!), and despite having 20 people on our payroll, it felt like the weight of the entire business was on just the two of us. We were in the kind of burnout that made us wish for something as simple as a two-week vacation without the anxiety that the world would collapse if we weren't there to micromanage every detail.

And then, one day, a surgeon we had worked with approached us with an offer. She wanted us to partner on a second location—a place that would not only perform surgeries but also have luxury recovery rooms for overnight stays. On paper, it sounded like exactly the kind of opportunity that could launch us into the kind of financial freedom we had been dreaming of. After all, this was the dream: to grow, sell the business for a small fortune, and then travel the world, living the kind of glamorous life that only the richest clients we'd helped could ever imagine.

But in reality? The idea made me want to crawl under the nearest table and nap for a decade.

I was just over 30 at the time, Dale a few years older, but we had reached a pivotal moment—one of those times in life when the pressure of what you *think* you want collides with the exhaustion of what you've been doing. I knew exactly what I needed to do: I needed out. I didn't want to be tied to this chaos any longer. I wanted the predictability of corporate America—the 9-to-5 life where the hardest thing to worry about was a missed lunch break. I missed driving a car that hadn't been soaked in bodily fluids, and the idea of taking a vacation without feeling like the entire business would fall apart was *heaven*.

But Dale wasn't there yet. He was the dreamer, the optimist, the one who still believed we were on the edge of something great. He agreed we should consider selling but also argued that if we expanded just a bit more, we could hit that financial freedom we were so close to achieving. I knew what he was thinking. He had that gleam in his eye—the one that said, *we're this close to our big break*. It was the same gleam he had when we first got into this business, thinking it would be a stepping stone to something more.

But the dream wasn't just about selling the business anymore. It was about the freedom that came with it—the chance to live a life that didn't involve 24/7 worry, waking up to calls from surgeons at all hours, or dealing with clients who seemed to think they had signed up for servants at their disposal 24/7 rather than medical care and support. And yet, somehow, the dream was slipping away, like sand through the fingers of someone too exhausted to hold on.

Then, out of nowhere, like some divine intervention, I got a call from a recruiter. I hadn't even applied for the job, yet there he was on the other end, laying out a dream offer—salary, commissions, perks. The whole package. It was as though the universe had handed me an escape hatch from a life I couldn't escape fast enough.

And just like that, I made up my mind. The Monarch and I were officially done. I couldn't even be sentimental about it. It wasn't that I didn't love what we had built, it was just that I couldn't see myself continuing down this path any longer. I told Dale about my decision. He was supportive, though I could see the disappointment in his eyes. He would stay on, manage the place, and we'd start looking for a buyer.

Saying goodbye to The Monarch wasn't easy. We had created something amazing, the two of us. We had met some of the most incredible people along the way, many of whom became lifelong friends. Our staff—oh, our staff—was a team of absolute rock stars who believed in what we were doing and went above and beyond to make sure every client was cared for like family. It was hard to walk away from that. Some of them have gone on to bigger and better things, and we still keep in touch to this day, proudly watching them achieve greatness.

We eventually found a buyer, but when they made their intentions clear, it became apparent that we couldn't let it go like that. They didn't want our vision. They didn't want the high-end recovery that we were known for. No, they just wanted to buy the name and reputation so they could turn The Monarch into some sort of private pay, low-quality service that could have been done by any random person off the street. I couldn't stand the thought of it—of seeing everything we worked for turned into just another impersonal, mass-market operation. I convinced Dale to walk away, even though the offer was tempting. It was hard, but it was the right decision. We couldn't let it be watered down.

So, we closed the doors. And as much as it hurt, I don't regret it for a second. Sure, we received calls for years after, sometimes begging us to come back or offering to fund our next venture. But once that chapter closed, it was really, truly closed.

I wouldn't say it was the hardest thing we've ever done, but it was definitely up there. And I wouldn't change it for anything. We came out of it stronger, wiser, and more prepared for whatever surprises life could throw our way. It solidified our relationship, made us stronger as a team, and proved that no matter what, we could take on anything together.

So, where are we now, you ask? Well, I can't tell you that just yet. But I *can* tell you this: neither of us have lost our entrepreneur sprit but our next adventure most certainly will not be another Monarch Retreat. There will never be another Monarch Retreat. What we built there was incredible, and while it was an unforgettable chapter in our lives, we've turned the page. The future's out there, and while we may not know exactly what it looks like yet, we're ready for the next adventure–whatever it may be.

And honestly? We're okay with that. Because no matter what's next, it's not going to involve 20 people on the payroll, 800 clients, and a never-ending stream of guests expecting their faces and bodies to be perfect. No more bedazzled neck braces. No more spa days that come with a side of surgical recovery. We're free. And the world? It's all ours.

Made in the USA
Las Vegas, NV
08 January 2025

16086727R00085